LUNCHING WITH FATHER

For Our dear friend
Isabella
with love,

Mitzi

21st October. 1990.

Also by Mitzi McCall:
Interior With Figure, The Book Guild Ltd.

LUNCHING WITH FATHER

Mitzi McCall

The Book Guild Ltd.

Sussex, England

The Book Guild Ltd.
25 High Street,
Lewes, Sussex.

First published 1990
© Mitzi McCall 1990
Set in Baskerville
Typesetting by Hawks Phototypesetters Ltd.,
Copthorne, Sussex.
Printed in Great Britain by
Antony Rowe Ltd.,
Chippenham, Wiltshire.

British Library Cataloguing in Publication Data
McCall, Mitzi 1916-
    Lunching with father.
    1. Scottish paintings. McCall, Charles, 1907-1989
    I. Title
759.2911

ISBN 0 86332 491 6

CONTENTS

Acknowledgements

The Author wishes to thank Mr and Mrs Waddington for allowing their painting "The Diamond Dealer, Jermyn Street, 24x18", by Charles McCall ROI NEAC, to be used for the jacket cover.

The directors of Christie's for their generous gift of the colour plates.

John W. Keffer for his help and diligence in proof reading, and the reproduction of the paintings and drawings from his collection of McCall's work.

David Ingham for the photography. Also Kate Strange for the back jacket photo of the McCalls laughing.

Carol Biss, Douglas Quiggan and Deborah Breach, for their editorial help, and friendly co-operation.

For Mark and Sue Sharman as a tribute to their warm friendship to Charles over a long period, especially at the end of his life.

I

Invitation to London

Father was in a good mood, his blue eyes were twinkling. 'If you have no social engagements for Saturday morning, I should be delighted to take you to lunch. You will have to travel up to Town with me in the morning, and help me in the office until lunch-time.' I accepted with glee. The long Summer holidays of 1930 were beginning to become tedious. I found being thirteen a neither here nor there age. I rushed into the drawing-room. The French doors were open into the sunlit garden. Jane, my stepmother, was sitting in her favourite chintz-covered arm chair. The room was in soft shadow with the three sun-blinds drawn; three large rose-coloured Persian carpets covered the polished oak boards; little tripod tables were dotted about the room between the chintz sofas and chairs; Jane was sitting in the doorway by the grand piano.

'Jane, I have just been invited to lunch with Daddy, all by myself. None of the others are coming.' She smiled, her bright brown eyes hidden by the reading spectacles. Her hair tinged with grey was pinned up on her head with a curly fringe.

'I expect he thinks that now you are at boarding school you will know how to behave in a London restaurant.'

'What shall I wear?'

'I should wear your new red cotton dress, with the straw boater, as long as the weather stays fine. I will give you some fresh ribbons for your plaits'.

'I wish I could have them cut off.'

'Not until you are sixteen, then we shall see . . .'

The next morning I was up in good time, and dressed in the clothes Jane suggested, choosing my best pair of silk stockings and

9

the black patent court shoes with heels, so frowned on by Matron at school. I was bubbling with excitement as I ran downstairs to breakfast.

I was greeted by ferocious growls from the family wire-haired terrier called "Mickey". 'That dog's mental, he should be put down!' Jane calmly poured the tea. 'He knows you are late, that is why he growls.' The whole family was at the breakfast table, buried behind their various newspapers. My sister Joyce, always called "Jo", was beside me. She was eighteen years old, very attractive with short blonde curly hair, but very unsociable in the mornings. Father sat at the head of the table, reading *The Times*. Then Marjorie, a brunette with long hair pinned up in plaits. She wore glasses, her figure was the envy of us all, and she was twenty. My eldest sister, Iris, always called "Cherry", completed the circle. She was twenty-two and worked for a vet. She was a great reader of novels, historic and romantic family sagas, and had not much interest in dress.

Father lowered his paper. 'Jane will be driving us to the station in five minutes, so be ready.' We arrived at Bickley station in time, and ran down the stairs as the great steam train thundered into the station. I had bought a third-class ticket, Father travelled first-class. 'Come into my carriage, it is always empty on Saturdays. If the inspector comes I will pay the excess.' It was a great treat to travel first-class, with carpets on the floor, and large tapestry seats with white antimacassars for one's head. I watched the backs of the little houses flash past the window. Some had very pretty gardens. I studied Father. He really did look very distinguished: his thick silver hair above his strong face, with high cheek bones, and a large nose, which his Jewish friends affectionately told him was the only reason he could hold his own in a trade that was becoming dominated by them.

We arrived at Holborn Viaduct station. As we passed the great steam engine, Father raised his hat to the engine driver, who said, 'See you've got company today, sir!'

'Yes, my youngest daughter. She is lunching with me.'

'Enjoy yourselves,' he said with a cheery wave.

As we left the station some ragged boys with bare feet were running through the dark entrance. Father looked severe. 'There's no need for that. We were poor enough as children, but we were always clean and well shod.'

Soon we were in Hatton Garden. Father always walked quickly, and I had to run a few steps to keep up with him. At No. 25 we climbed the stairs to the office on the first floor. A glass door had printed on it:

JERWOOD & WARD
DEALERS IN PEARLS & PRECIOUS STONES

With a great jangle of keys the door was unfastened, revealing a large office with two windows and two baize-covered tables which stood sideways into the room. The floor was covered with grey fitted carpet and Persian rugs, and chairs were either side of the tables. Two enormous black safes stood in the corner, and a shelf with a jeweller's scales was the other side of the fireplace. Father removed his grey trilby hat which went with his "Saturday grey suit", and placed it on the mahogany hatstand.

'Now you go through to the back office, and when people come in, leave them in the little hall, only opening the glass trap to see who is there and call me.'

Several dealers called, all rather sportingly dressed for Saturday, and Mr Roberts, a stone-cutter, or lapidary, who always looked worried. Jerwood and Ward were principally pearl merchants, shipping a million pounds worth of pearls a year to New York, for distribution through America.

The morning soon passed. I was called into the front office, 'Come and look at this.' Father held in his hands a beautiful cross. 'It is cut out of solid emerald, there are no joins, and it has diamond trefoils at the ends. It once belonged to the Queen of Spain.'

'Oh Daddy, it's gorgeous. 'What is it worth?'

He grinned, his eyes twinkling. 'A King's ransom, I shall have to think of a price!'

'When I grow up I shall have emeralds.'

He laughed, 'Let's go to lunch.'

The taxi arrived at "Kettners", a restaurant in Soho, and we went into a narrow hall. I was introduced to the head waiter, a Monsieur Rubicon, and Mr Meyer, the manager. Then Father took me into the bar, which was small and intimate. We sat down at a table near the window. In the distance one could hear a barrel organ churning out "Lily of Laguna".

'What would you like for a cocktail?'

'May I have a Bronx?'

It was produced with great showmanship by the barman who poured it out of the cocktail shaker, and it foamed in the glass, and tasted delicious. Father sipped his dry Martini. 'How was the first term at school?'

'It was rather rough, I nearly gave up, mostly because I was in the wrong House. All my friends were in West House, and I was sharing a two-room with a Senior, which meant I was asleep when she came to bed. It was very lonely. However at her end of term "chat" the Headmistress, Miss Davies, suggested I should move to West House next term where I would be with my friends in a dormitory. So I think my troubles are over!'

'It is a good thing to stick things out when the going is rough. In my youth, it was very hard and when conditions improve one appreciates it. At a school like yours you will find you gain an indefinable something, already you have the beginnings of it.'

At that moment the manager appeared to lead us into lunch. The dining-room was a series of small rooms leading one into the other. Our table was in the end room in a window corner. The other tables were full. I noticed some well-known faces, actors, and politicians. We settled in at the table and the meal was ordered, with teasing from father about my love of pork sausages! A half bottle of white wine was requested and at last the meal was under way.

'Daddy, would you tell me about your childhood. I have only heard scraps?'

He took a sip of wine. 'It's quite a story. The first I can remember is running through a large house my father had bought in Tottenham, and pulling all the bell-ropes, causing a frightful clatter! Of course I was caught and my ears soundly boxed!'

'Were your parents very strict?'

'My father was, mind you we were eight in family. Walter was the eldest, then Will and Albert, followed by Edward and me, and Arthur was the youngest, with two girls, Charlotte and Bessie, so it needed a great deal of discipline to keep that lot in order! Mother was a gentle soul. She lost several babies. I always reckoned she had about fourteen children!'

'Didn't she know?'

'Well, she had so much to do, in the end it was hard for her to remember! She was a saint in my eyes. What she put up with from the Old Man, a brilliant business man, but a drinker and a gambler. He once owned the site of "Harrods", then had to sell to pay his horse racing debts.'

'Where did you go to school?'

'A small primary school in Holloway. I was lucky because we

St. James's Boys School 1889, Freddie Ward is fourth from right, front row

had a marvellous class teacher. He said, 'You boys have not long enough at school to have any frills, so you have to learn fast.

Reading, Writing and Arithmetic. He proceeded to give us mental arithmetic every morning, quick as a flash all round the class. His philosophy was to have a firm ground of fundamental knowledge, and go to night school for the rest.'

'Gosh Daddy! I could do with him now, my maths are frightful!'

It was time for our delicious Peach Melba, Father laughed at my delight.

'How long were you at school?'

'Well I stayed until I was twelve, but I went to work at eight!'

'I don't believe you!'

'It's the truth. It came about in a strange way. I told Arthur, my younger brother, I had found a way to make us some pocket money, and we went to the newsagent and took a load of evening papers, and hopped on and off the trams selling them. All went well until I jumped onto a tram, and there was the Old Man! He was furious, and grabbed us by the collar, and took us home, where we were both given "six of the best". I felt guilty for little Arthur, as it was my fault. The next day I was sent for to father's study.

Edward, Fred and
Arthur Ward. 1894

'You want to earn money? Right I have fixed you up with Mr Briggs the butcher, you will go with him to Smithfield at 5 am and unload the meat!'

Mother dressed me warmly in a thick jersey, woolly cap, and I went out into the dark winter morning. Mr Brigg's shop was round the corner from our house. The lights were on in his yard and he came out of his back door.

'Good morning, Fred, I hear you want to help me load the meat, and earn yourself some money!'

'Good morning, sir. Yes, I should like to earn some money!'

'Right, put your foot on the wheel hub and pull yourself up by the rail. You will sit beside me, there's not much of you!'

Mr Briggs was a bluff rosy-cheeked man with side-whiskers, sturdily built, but not tall. I sat beside him behind the two horses pulling the van, their brown hides gleaming in the street lights, and we set off with a clatter through the City for Smithfield.

We arrived to flaring gaslights and another world, of white-coated men with bloodstained overalls and great carcasses of meat on hooks. It took us an hour to load the meat. Mr Briggs helped me with the larger carcasses, but the lambs and smaller pieces I managed. There were remarks about the size of his assistant but considering the roughness of the meat porters, they were very kind. It was bitterly cold, and I must have looked frozen, because Mr Briggs took me with him into a tavern, and bought a tot of rum.

'Here you are lad. You look blue with cold, that'll warm you!'

It certainly did! and for the first time in my life I knew what it was to feel tipsy. I had to hold on to the seat rails. The buildings were spinning round. We unloaded the meat at the shop, and Mr Briggs gave me a sixpence.

'Thank you, sir.'

'You did well, Fred, see you at 5 am tomorrow.'

I found it difficult to imagine my father as a child younger than myself and the thought that he had been encouraged to work so hard for so little money upset me. I could not help interrupting his story.

'Daddy, it's horrifying, how could they let a little boy do a job like that?'

'It was Victorian England, life was very hard for the working-class.'

Mr Meyer had brought some petit fours for our coffee.

'Did you enjoy your meal, Mr Ward?'

'Yes indeed, the best lunch in London for three shillings and sixpence!'

'Well you know we do it as an attraction for people to return for our more elaborate dinners at seven and sixpence.'

'Cheap at double the price!' said Father with a broad grin.

'And Mademoiselle, how was your lunch?'

'The cat's whiskers'

Mr Meyer and M. Rubicon (who had just come up to the table) looked puzzled.

'*Les moustaches du chat!*' I said in my school-girl French. They all rocked with laughter.

'I shall not let you forget that!' said Mr Meyer, who escorted us to the door. The taxi was waiting, and I waved "Goodbye" as we left for Victoria station.

2

It was three months later, in the Christmas holidays, I had my
next invitation to lunch. At last I had persuaded Jane to let me cut
off my pigtails and unfortunately she insisted upon accompanying
me to the hairdressers. Jane could be a real dragon and when her
ewe-lamb was about to be shorn, she was very much on the
warpath. I saw the glint in her eye and feared the worst. A rather
gangling young man with a rather superior manner appeared in
the cubicle. Jane went into the attack.

'I don't want her hair cut too short, and I want the plaits back!'

'Very well, modom. What are you doing to do with them, put
them in a glass case?'

'There's no need to be impudent.'

'I want them for her to have should she ever want a hair-piece
in the future.'

By now hate was thick in the air. I was intensely miserable, with
scarlet cheeks, and very embarrassed. He cut off each pigtail still
plaited and sent the junior for a bag, and gave the hair to Jane
with a flourish. I sat staring at myself with the grotesque sprouts of
hair, sticking out each side of my ears.

'What shall we do now, modom?' He said with obvious sarcasm.

Jane was very cross. 'Just cut it into a bob, and we shall leave.
You do not seem to have much idea of style.'

He did just that and it looked ghastly, like Greta Garbo on a
very bad day! I was so near to tears that my usual fighting spirit
was lacking. All I wanted was to get away and hide. We returned
home, Jane in a rage, 'I told you it would not suit you, you'll have
to let it grow!'

There was no point in arguing. It *did* look dreadful. I was
marched into the drawing-room. Father was just home, and Jo and

Marjorie were sitting there with him. 'Look what that awful man has done. Doesn't she look a sight!'

Father looked most uncomfortable, and obviously agreed with Jane, my sisters roared with laughter. I turned and rushed upstairs to my bedroom, sobbing my heart out. There was a tap, on the door, and Jo came in, 'Don't cry, I will take you to my man tomorrow. It only needs styling, nobody could look good the way your hair has been cut. We will go together, and leave Jane safely at home.'

'Oh Jo, thank you. I thought I had made a dreadful mistake.'

The next day we went to Jo's hairdresser, who washed and cut my hair into a good shape, and curled the ends.

'There, you see you look very nice.'

'Your sister has lovely thick hair. It is very easy to style. I fear the man yesterday, was just being malicious because he was angry!'

'Thank you so much. It does look nice I shall always come here.'

We emerged elated with the success of our venture, and went to the local café to celebrate. I had Jo in gales of laughter describing the battle between Jane and the hairdresser. All my grief forgotten, now I had a reasonable appearance!

Jo said, 'Now I have helped you, will you come to my rescue?'

'Of course I will, if I can.'

'Marjorie and I want to invite certain people to her twenty-first dance in January, and Jane is being very strict about the list. Could you persuade her to let us write our list of guests, then give her suggestions? Otherwise we shall end up with the usual boring parental friends. You can always wind her round your little finger.'

'That will be difficult, she's not stupid. She was not bad about our fancy-dress last year, why are you so worried?'

'Well, she does not want to invite Leo, and thinks Larry and his friends should not be invited as they have not returned our hospitality.'

I understood in a flash. It was their boyfriends they were worried about, both on the parental blacklist! I promised to do what I could. When father returned that evening he was relieved and delighted with my new look.

'We must celebrate, come and lunch with me next Saturday.'

The next day I was very pleasant to Jane, and offered to go shopping with her, which pleased her. The morning went well, and as we were driving back in the car I said, 'Jane, do you think we could have our own guest list for Marjorie's party? You could vet it, and add your own guests; it would be much more fun not to have so many older people and relatives.'

'You have been put up to this. I suspect it is the others who want it.'

'Well, honestly we all want it. It seems such a shame to have the wonderful dance floor in the drawing-room, and not have enough young people to make a good dance, especially as you are having the little three-piece band again.'

'Well, I must ask your Father.'

I rushed round the house looking for Jo who was writing in the dining-room.

'Jo, she's going to ask Daddy if we can have our list!

'Gosh, that's quick work, I knew you could do it.'

'We have to make out the lists of guests, we are limited to seventy.'

'I only care about one person anyway.'

'Old snooty-drawers I suppose?'

'Yes, if you want to be rude. He isn't the least bit snooty when you know him.'

'He is to me.'

'It's only because you are young. anyway, thank you for working the oracle, I shall have to get Marjorie to help me make the list.'

The next morning being Saturday, I was ready to go to London with Father. We travelled first-class as previously.

'Daddy, has Jane asked you abut the invitation list for Marjorie's twenty-first birthday?'

He looked surprised 'First I've heard of it.'

'Oh well, I had better leave it to her.'

It was rather busy in the office. A cable was waiting his attention from Allie Osterwald in New York, and we had to stay late in order to telephone him. Father agreed the deal with him, which put him in a sparkling mood for lunch.

'We shall go to the "L'Ecu de France" in Jermyn Street, and celebrate selling a bunch of pearls for £250,000.' It was much more impressive than "Kettner's" restaurant, although secretly I preferred the friendliness of the latter, but the food was delicious. We had lobster mayonnaise, and boeuf à la Bourguignonne. We had some very dry white wine with the lobster, and I asked father to continue the story of his youth that he had started to tell me during our previous outing and I had been horrified to hear him describe the way he had been treated. He had dismissed my worries by reminding me that he had been brought up in Victorian England, when things were different.

'As I told you life was very basic, but I found I was able to memorise poetry and prose very easily. I went to St. James' Boys' Sunday School, and was able to recall any passage they asked me from the Bible, and won the "Arthur Stocks Memorial Prize" which was a Bible. Inside was an inscription in gold, "Presented to F. WARD 1896." I was twelve years old, and very proud of my prize. As I left the church hall in my Sunday suit, I saw a group of boys waiting for me led by the school bully. I quickly gave the valued book to Arthur who was behind me and said, 'Run for it out of the side door!'

'Give us yer Bible then or I'll give yer a bloody nose!'

I squared up to this big bully and we had such a fight that there was blood everywhere!

It was brought to a halt by the Sunday School master.

'Stop this fighting at once! I am surprised at you, Fred Ward, just gaining the Memorial Prize, I have a good mind to confiscate it. Now all go home before I cane you.'

'Oh, Daddy how unfair. What did they say at home?'

'When I got home Arthur had prepared them for the worst. Of course I was in a frightful pickle, blood all over my face, and mud on my best suit. My Father was very angry.

The next day he sent for me and I thought 'Gor blimey' another belting, but I was wrong.

'Right Fred, its's time you went to work. I have apprenticed you to a jeweller on Ludgate Hill. His name is Mr Evans and he will pay you two shillings and sixpence a week, and your keep. You will come home Sundays and give mother a shilling for your clothes. Be ready at eight tomorrow with your bag packed, and I will take you to the shop.'

The waiter came with the Boeuf Bourguignon, and Father had ordered a bottle of Nuit St. Georges. It was all so luxurious that it made the story of his childhood even more extraordinary. The contrast between his life then and now was so great!

'The next morning, my father and I set out in the chilly October morning by tramcar. Mother had been a little upset and I was apprehensive. Father sat beside me on the tram as it rattled and clanked along the line, full of men going to offices, in high starched collars and dark suits. His face was very stern. He was very like King Edward VII in appearance, and I read the signs to keep quiet.

We went into a small jeweller's shop on Ludgate hill. The lights were on in the window, which was full of brooches, rings and

Thomas Ward, Freddie's Father

Freddie Ward 1932

silver-plated articles. Mr Evans was behind the counter and greeted my father warmly.

'Good morning, Mr Ward, so this is the lad."

'Yes, this is Fred. He has a good report from school, he can read, and writes a neat hand, and is very good at arithmetic.'

'Right, Fred, come with me and I will show you where to put your things.'

Father said, 'I shall not stop. Come home to lunch on Sunday, work hard and do what Mr Evans tells you.'

With that he turned on his heels and left us.

Mr Evans was rather portly, with a red face, a heavy gold Albert watchchain hung across his stomach. He picked up a key and locked the shop door.

'Now lad, pick up your basket, and I'll show you where to stow your belongings.'

I followed him into a hall, with a short flight of stairs, a gas lamp lighting a wide landing. Facing us was a large cupboard. Evans opened the doors. Inside was a wall bed, with a shelf at the end.

'Put your basket on the shelf; this is where you sleep!'

Once again, I found it hard to believe that my own father had been treated so badly. I could not stay silent for another moment.

'I don't believe it, Daddy. It sounds just like Dickens!'

'Well, it is God's truth. You must remember Dickens was a reporter, and he knew his London. It was very tough going for working boys in those days. Mr Evans then took me up to the first floor to meet Mrs Evans. She was a thin worn woman, rather untidy, but she gave me a warm smile.

'This is Fred, he is my new apprentice. I have shown him his place, you must tell him his duties. Send him down to the shop when you have finished.'

He disappeared down the stairs. I must have looked rather scared.

'Don't be afraid, Fred. He is a hard master, but not unkind. I am always here if you want any help. I shall wake you at six in the morning, you will go down and take down the shutters, (they are very heavy), then come up to the kitchen for breakfast. Then clean the shop. You must always be clean in the shop, so keep a clean shirt for that. I will wash your clothing. You will work in the shop from 8.30 to mid-morning, when I will give you a sandwich. Then you work through until the shop closes at 8 o'clock in the evening. You will then change and put up the shutters, and I shall give you some supper before you go to bed.'

Father's narrative was interrupted by the sweet trolley which was rolling up to the table.

'What would you like to eat, Mademoiselle?'

I have never been able to eat a lot of rich food, so turned my eyes away from the tempting cream gateaux and trifles, and chose the sliced oranges with caramel shredded peel, in Grand Marnier liqueur. Father had his favourite cheese instead.

After we had eaten, I wanted to hear more.

'How long did you stand it?'

'Well there was no question of leaving, one had to have a good reference to get another job, so I had to serve my three years apprenticeship. It was a tough job. Mrs Evans, his wife, was a very worn creature, but very good to me, often slipping a jam sandwich into my hand, and a quick cup of cocoa on the bitter winter mornings. Evans was a heavy drinker, and would return from the pub on Saturday nights much the worse for wear. He would then beat up his wife, and I would pull the pillow over my ears to shut out her cries. After several weeks of this I could stand it no longer, and went to their room and pulled him off her.

'If you don't leave her alone I'll get a policeman!' He was so surprised that he stopped.

'What a brute!' I said.

'It was the demon drink. My father died of it. He was drinking a bottle of brandy a day. It was very cheap then. Strangely, I was the one he sent for when he was dying. He said, 'Make sure I get a seat in the front row, Fred. I like to hear the trams go by! You are the only one I trust to do it.'

'What did he mean?' I asked.

'He wanted a grave in the front of the cemetery, not a quiet place at the back!'

The strange humour of a grandfather I had never known made me quiet for a moment. I vaguely understood that father had inherited more than a sense of humour from his father. They had both shared an openness which tempted me to ask about something which had puzzled me for several years.

'Is that why you teach all of us to drink from an early age? Some of my friends' parents are very shocked when I say I have drinks.'

'Yes I reckon that if you know what you are drinking, and are allowed a glass or two, you will not go wild when I am not about! Also you will appreciate how much you can drink without bad effects. I should say *you* have my head for drink. You seem to manage it very well!'

We were sipping our coffee when Father said, 'Do your sisters confide in you?'

'Not a great deal. Jo is starting to tell me a few things. I think she is very keen on Larry. I don't like him, but she says I am too young to know.'

He looked thoughtful. 'I am most worried about Marjorie. That chap Leo is married. She says he tells her it's over, but I do not like the fellow. I tell Jane to keep quiet. I am so afraid she will run off with him, then the fat would be in the fire!'

I did not really understand fully what he meant, but I thought about it going back on the train.

3

Christmas in Shawfield House

Christmas, 1930 was almost upon us and the house was buzzing with activity, with great rustlings of paper, and cries of 'don't come in!'

John Fuller, the gardener, wheeled his barrow full of holly to the front door. A great white dust sheet covered the hall carpet, and the holly and mistletoe were placed on it. Father was in charge of decorations, (in case we marked the wallpaper!) Fuller went up the ladder, and Papa gave his orders. Great coloured paper chains were hung in festoons in the drawing-room, and the evergreens were pushed behind all the pictures and mirrors. Then the mistletoe was strategically placed, in the hall and just inside the drawing-room. A great iron basket glowed in the fireplace, full of coals and logs. It all looked very festive. The bay at the end of the drawing-room had a false window of looking glass, which reflected all the colour and glitter in the room. Father said, 'Come on girls, now the house is decorated it is time to go shopping and help me choose your presents.'

We all rushed to get our hats and coats.

Cherry was rather indignant, 'I don't like to know what I am getting!'

'Oh don't fuss. We shall help him buy yours when you aren't looking.'

It was great fun shopping with Father. He always flirted outrageously with the shop assistants, and loved to buy us pretty lingerie. He bought a beautiful pink pleated nightdress for Jane. She was teased unmercifully about it, and pretended to be rather shocked at our suggestive remarks. We all had lovely things and returned home in great spirits.

It was our job to wrap the gifts for him, then all the presents were placed in heaps, and put into old pillow cases suitably labelled. There was one for each of the staff, and it was quite a business sorting them all out, especially as Cherry's labels always came adrift. The final task was to place them at the end of each person's bed, taking the gardener's sacks to the cottage.

Appetising aromas crept through from the kitchen, where Jane and Mrs Frisby, the cook, were finishing the preparation for the Christmas lunch. We had guests coming, although to see the food, one would have expected at least a regiment! The top of the spinet was covered with a cloth and had dishes of fruit, nuts and raisins, dates, and the Christmas cake in all its splendour.

The whole house was awake early. I heard Jane go downstairs to make sure the turkey had been put into the oven. I pulled my sack of presents onto the bed. It was a good Christmas and there were no disappointments. I rushed across the landing to Marjorie's and Jo's large bedroom. Marjorie and Jo were in high spirits. I heard excited voices as I opened the door. 'Happy Christmas!' and we hugged and kissed each other.

'I loved the green purse you gave me, Jo, it will look so nice with my new dress, and thank you, Marjorie, for the lovely fizzy bath-salts.'

'Look what we have had. Did you ever see so many things?'

Leo has given Marjorie a special brooch made like an amaryllis'

'Why an amaryllis?'

'Marjorie gave me one of her shy secretive looks.

'We both love the book *The Secret Garden*. It's part of that, too involved to explain now. Don't you think it's pretty? I am thrilled with it.'

'What did you have, Jo?'

She looked up from all the coloured paper and string, her large brown eyes alive with excitement in her heart-shaped face.

'A beautiful pair of pants from Daddy, such fine satin they won't show a wrinkle under my new slinky evening-dress!'

At that point Cherry entered the room dragging two sacks of presents.

'Happy Christmas! I've come to show you my presents.'

We all groaned. Cherry's friends were legion, and they all gave her boring gifts, (in our eyes) which we had to try to enjoy inspecting!

Marjorie said, 'Not now Cherry, there isn't time, we are going to church, and have to be back by twelve as the "Uncles" are coming in for a drink.'

Shawfield House

Looking rather put out she departed, dragging her sacks back to her room.

'We will look at them later, after tea.' She cheered up at once.

We went to St Nicolas Church in Chislehurst, joining in the carols and enjoying the Christmas service. It put us all in a very festive mood. When we returned to Shawfield House it looked so beautiful with the lights on in all the rooms, and a sprinkling of snow over the garden. As Father drove the car up the drive, Jo said, 'I am so glad you bought this house , Daddy, we must surely be happy here.'

'It will not be my fault if you aren't.' He gave a broad grin.

We all scrambled out of the car. I went along the passage to the kitchen, where Jane was very busy. Cook had on a large white apron covering her ample bosom, her face was red from the heat of the oven, and the kitchen table was covered with pies and all manner of things.

'Happy Christmas, Mrs Frisby!'

She beamed. 'Thank you , Miss Mitzi, for the lovely box of soap, I shall put it between my sheets. Makes 'em smell nice!'

'Now Mitzi, don't come in here chattering. We are too busy, go and join the others.'

Cook gave me a wink, and I beat a retreat.

The "Uncles" arrived on the dot of twelve. They were not blood relations, but had always lived in the house opposite us. They were great fun, all with white hair and white moustaches, which tickled when they kissed us. We were all given the usual box of chocolates each, and were bombarded with questions. The champagne was handed round, and "Happy Christmas" was the toast.

'Have you been to church?'

'Yes, Father took us, poor Jane had to help Cook. We have guests for lunch, so are having the main feast early.'

'How is Rebecca?' (She was their devoted servant, very old school, with a bun on top of her head. Very stern with us as children.)

Uncle John, the eldest brother, replied, 'Sadly her rheumatism is bad, she's getting on like us all!'

'Come on, Uncle John, you know you are going to marry me when I am old enough!'

'Well, you had better grow up fast, I am seventy-five, and Willie is seventy-three, and Charles is seventy!'

I looked at him with astonishment. Seventy seemed so very old.

At that moment there was a fresh outburst of greetings, Auntie Eva, had arrived with her little daughter Eve, aged four. Then all our lunch-time guests crowded in. Gladys Hatherill, Father's very attractive secretary, arrived with her fiancé Francis, her sister Winifred and her medical student fiancé, Reggie, and their widowed mother. For a while it was utter confusion, then the "Uncles" car arrived to take them to their celebrations, and Jane said would we all go through to the dining-room for the Christmas feast.

The dining-room was really my favourite room in the house. It was as large as the drawing-room, furnished in soft blues, Prussian blue velvet curtains, an enormous Persian carpet covered the floor, coloured in soft blues and greys. The great mahogany table, which measured twenty feet, stood in the centre of the room, the large carved grape and ball legs holding the array of silver and glass. With much laughter and excitement we were all seated. I was beside Jane at the far end of the room, Father was at the head of the table, between Auntie Eva and Mrs Hatherill. It took ages to eat lunch. We finally reached the coffee and liqueurs. Jane never drank, it really did not agree with her, but on Christmas Day, she always had a cherry brandy! We would all watch with delight while the drink took its very swift effect. Father enjoyed it, her eyes would sparkle, and then she would find everything very amusing, and roar with laughter.

We all settled round the fire, and Gladys said 'I have always wanted to ask you Mr Ward, how did Jerwood and Ward start?'

Father smiled, 'It is quite a long story, are you sure you want to hear it?'

Auntie Eva asked to be excused, as she wanted to take Eve for her rest, and Jo left the room with her. Jane went to check on the staff, and see they had everything for their festivities. The rest of us waited for him to begin.

Father had told me the story of his early childhood, up until the time he was apprenticed to Mr Evans, a jeweller on Ludgate Hill. He now had quite an audience for what I knew would be an interesting tale. Father was a natural storyteller.

Father's Story

(I actually found this written down by Freddie in his papers after death) *It is his story —*

I had finished my apprenticeship, and a friendly dealer showed me an advertisement for a manager in a leading City shop. I was fifteen and I managed to get some errands to do in the City that morning. It was an impressive shop, near the Bank of England, with a magnificent stock of jewellery and silver. I entered the carpeted showroom and a large man rose from a desk with a lamp on it. He had a kindly face, and his eyes smiled behind his glasses. He wore a morning suit.

'Yes, my boy, what do you want?'

I drew myself up as tall as possible.

'Please, sir, I should like to see you about the manager's job!'

'You look rather young for a manager!'

I grinned. 'That's what the colour-sergeant said when I tried to serve in the South African war.' He said, "Go home and tell your mother to give you more treacle pudding!" but honestly, sir, I could do the job. I have been working for Mr Evans on Ludgate Hill, apprenticed for three years. He pays very badly, and I am anxious to get on.'

Percy Davidson regarded me thoughtfully.

'I was told to come by Mr Harris who thought I would be suitable.'

'When could you start?'

'Next Monday, sir.'

'I shall give you a month's trial, I shall need three character references, and you must wear a morning suit!'

We all laughed.

Father smiled. 'It seems absurd today, but no one of any importance wore anything else in business before the Great War.

To cut a long story short, I had the suit made by an East End tailor and, complete with silk-hat, presented myself for work the next Monday.

That night, to celebrate my luck, I was getting thirty shillings a week, I went to the Tivoli Music Hall in The Strand. There was a large commissionaire on the door, with a huge moustache. He took a quick look at me in my new morning suit and silk-hat, and said, 'Good evening M'Lord!' It made my evening.

I worked very hard, all the "Nobs" of the City came to the shop, I was always straight with them, and I soon was making Mr Davidson a good profit a week.

One of the most attractive *demi-mondaines* of the town, called Jennie Wild, would come in with an important City gentleman, and choose a nice piece of jewellery. The next day I was sent to her flat to buy it back, less 10%. She was in again with a different fellow, and bought the same piece, same thing happened. She came in again with a third and again the same brooch was purchased. This time she kept it, then they all thought they had given it to her! In fact two of the gentlemen fought a duel over her in Hyde Park! It was a great scandal at the time.

Another fellow came into the shop, big and blustery. 'My man, I wish to purchase a silver dinner-service, I own the bank round the corner.' He gave me his card. I knew the bank, a small place, there were a lot of them in those days.

'Right, sir, I shall need a deposit, and cash on delivery.'

'Here are three sovereigns, I shall give you the rest on delivery.'

I went the next morning with the service. He was standing at the back of the bank, and came forward when he saw me.

'May I have the balance of seventeen sovereigns?'

'I do not think there is that much hurry, is there?'

'Sorry sir, it is the rule of the shop, cash on delivery.'

He grew very red in the face. The cashier looked very scared.

'Open the till and show him our sovereigns!'

The clerk went very red in the face and opened the till and it was empty.

'I am sorry, sir, I cannot leave the silver service.'

'Show him the silver drawer!'

That was empty too!

Cherry's Christening 1908 — Back row, from left. Aunt Eva, Father, Grandfather Ashley-Cooper and Jane. Sitting: Grandmother Ashley-Cooper and Mama, holding Cherry

I just picked up the box and walked out.

He was made bankrupt the next week.

It was a much better life working for Davidson, I had been watching the dealers as they brought in the goods, and learnt quite a bit about dealing. By this time I had met and married Lilian. My wife loved extravagant and pretty things. Her mother said the only reason she married me was because I gave her a beautiful silk parasol, and she was told she could only accept such a gift from her fiancé. Her idea of a night out was a hansom-cab to the theatre, dinner, and home by cab along The Embankment. It often took a week's pay. In no time we had two children, and Lizzie the maid to look after them. When Marjorie was born in 1910 I tried to make some money on the stock market but sadly lost the lot. I went to a small clock maker I knew. I told him I had been foolish, but if he would lend me £25 I knew of some cheap cuckoo clocks, on which he was certain to double his money, and would he lend me a further £25 to buy my wife a diamond ring, because she was having a baby! He was tickled by my cheek, and gave me the money. We did so well with the clocks I was able to repay him at once. He was very pleased with the business.

I had asked Mr Davidson to let me have £200 in the till to use for dealing. In a month I turned it into £2,000. He was very pleased. My salary was £3 per week. I asked for a rise.

'No Fred, I cannot afford it.'

A man called William H Crane came into the shop to buy a small jewel.

I was fascinated by him. He was a man of medium height, immensely broad and heavily built with a large beard. His eyes were brown in colour and brilliant. He was immaculately dressed, well-spoken with a slight Canadian accent. We chatted and he told me tales of his travels all over the world, we became friendly, and one day he invited me to dine with him. It was the summer of 1909. He dined me lavishly with wine, ending with cigars. The dinner must have cost him three weeks of my wages! He said that he was a man of importance in the insurance world, and was looking for someone to run his London office. He asked me what I was earning. When I said I was earning the shop £7,000 *per annum*, but only getting £150 in salary a year, he immediately offered me £500 a year plus commission. The condition was that I should read and learn enough about insurance to take over his business in six months!

The following months were the hardest I ever knew. Late into the night I studied the extraordinary ramifications of insurance. At last I felt confident that I could leave my secure job, and take over W H Crane & Company in his absence. His plan was to leave his wife nominally in charge. (She was a nondescript character, who I shrewdly suspected had no marriage lines.) After a month she was to join her husband in Canada.

My excitement rose at the thought of the wealth in store, but an inner caution kept nagging away that there must be some snag I could not see!

I asked Crane if I could be present at a meeting with his clients, and witness the actual negotiations, and gain experience of his methods. After some demur he agreed.

One night he invited me to his office. A couple of the most villainous ruffians came into the office, obviously from the Eastern Mediterranean. They wished to insure a ship from Athens to some port on the African coast, and a great battle took place over the rates to be paid. With the knowledge I had already gained, I would not have insured the ship for five pounds. The sum being discussed was £100,000! The deal was finally settled, the premium paid in cash, and the policy issued. Everyone was happy except me.

When they had left the office, Crane turned to me, 'What would you have done in my place?'

'I would not have insured that old tub for a pound, and thrown those clients of yours out of the office!'

I could not understand why he had issued them with a policy. I had often worked in his magnificent suite of offices in Queen Victoria Street, late into the night, and seen clients go in and out until quite late, but this was the first business meeting I had witnessed.

Crane turned to me with a smile. 'That's where you are making a big mistake! I have the premium. They will find it a different matter to establish a loss.'

I was deeply disturbed. I thought I could see the ultimate result: to collect as many premiums as fast as possible, delay all claims, even by litigation, and eventually disappear with the loot! I decided to call Crane's bluff.

He was offering me £500 *per annum,* on a five year contract, plus commission on all premiums. I offered to start in one month's time if he would give me £2,500 as a down payment. (Which was a mere pittance according to his suggestion of the money I was going to make). He flew into a great rage and threatened to shoot me, he had a loaded revolver in his desk, but I remained adamant, and we finally parted.

I was bitterly disappointed to see my dreams of wealth fade. The sequel was as I feared. Another man took the job and was paid a month's salary. The "wife" was left stranded in London, and Crane disappeared with all the funds. The palatial office was reclaimed by the landlord, the staff left unpaid, and the furnishings returned to the hirers.

My third daughter, Joyce, was born in 1912. My salary was still only three pounds a week, *I needed to earn more money.*

A young dealer had been coming to the shop, he was charming, well educated, and had good connections.

He told me he had the chance of a fine suite of offices on Holborn Viaduct, but was unable to afford the rent on his own. He was looking for a partner, was I interested? His name was Edward Jerwood.

I said 'We could call our firm "Jerwood & Ward".

'That sounds splendid!'

We both laughed and shook hands on the agreement.

'I shall enjoy working with you, shall we start in the New Year?'

There was a momentary silence, everyone had been listening

Edward Jerwood

intently, then a clamour of voices, questioning Father on various points. Francis said 'I am astounded at your courage to step out into the unknown, and have the confidence that you could make it work!'

Gladys chipped in, 'It is unbelievable Mr Ward that you should have worked "Jerwood & Ward" into the great business you have today!'

Father looked very happy, and I was proud to have him as my Father.

There was a clatter as tea was brought in, with a large Christmas cake to be devoured! We all settled down to the marathon of Christmas eating.

4

The Party

The Christmas holiday was soon over, and the preparations began for Marjorie's twenty-first birthday party on the twentieth of January. Jane took us all to London to buy our dresses for the event. We went to a small dress shop off Oxford Street, an old favourite of my sisters. Cherry fell in love with a green net dress, the skirt sprinkled with sequins, and very expensive. Jane said it was unsuitable, and too much money. Easy-going Cherry could be very stubborn on occasions and insisted in trying it on. Much to our surprise it looked quite good. She looked pleadingly at Jane, who gave in. Jo's choice was beige lace cut on the cross and flaring out at the knees, with which she planned to wear father's Christmas present of green jade, necklace and earrings, with shoes to match. I was allowed my first long evening-dress. The most simple one was flame chiffon. I was very excited. Jane had a brocade in browns, which suited her very well. We all returned home delighted with our shopping. As Marjorie was working in father's office, she went with her friend Gladys during her lunch hour. She chose white and silver lamé, with a very low back, and décolleté front. She looked marvellous in it. (Jane said it was too low and she would catch her death of cold!) We all laughed and said she was old-fashioned. Father's birthday present was a pearl necklace.

Cherry was late again for dinner and Jane was cross. 'I shall ring up that vet, she is always keeping us waiting for dinner.'

The next evening we were told, 'I have been invited by Clifford (The vet) to go to tea with him in the country.'

She was clearly very excited. 'It is to make up for keeping me late at the surgery. He is coming to fetch me at 3 pm on Saturday.'

On Saturday Jane was sitting in the drawing-room. She rang for

35

Mary the house parlour maid. 'When Mr Davis comes, please show him in here.'

'Certainly, madam.'

The interview was conducted in utter privacy, none of us was allowed in the room. Cherry was sent for, and she and the vet left for their outing. When she returned we all asked what Jane had said. Cherry could hardly tell us for laughing.

'She asked him if his intentions towards me were honourable!'

We all collapsed laughing. To ask that man, a real rake if ever there was one . . . Strangely, he respected Jane for it, and never misbehaved with Cherry.

Jo had learnt to drive the MG sports car Father had given us for Christmas. It was very dashing, red and silver, a two-seater with a dickey. We loved it with the hood down.

'Like to come for a drive?'

'Yes please.'

So off we went into the Kentish countryside. It was very exciting, and we zoomed past our friendly AA man, (known as smiler) who looked rather startled. We were doing 70 mph! Jo asked me if I would like to go to Eastbourne on Saturday, she had asked Marjorie to come too, and it would give them both good practice in driving. I was to ride in the dickey.

Jo said, 'It's much more fun with you. Marjorie is always scared when I go over 40 mph, and this is a sports car. She is getting very secretive lately, I suppose it is her closeness with Leo.'

'Do you think he is getting a divorce?'

'It is not discussed, and Marjorie is very touchy on the subject.'

We returned home with ravenous appetites and cooked crumpets round the fire in the drawing-room.

We had a glorious day out on Saturday. The roads were empty as it was winter, and we came back at a great speed as we were all going to a party given by the vet, who lived in a local hotel. We changed quickly, and all four of us drove off to the party. We were rather shaken to find it was held in out host's bedroom! Even more so when we saw that most of the men were old, thirty at least, and the drinks were whiskey and gin. Jo whispered to me, 'A quick drink and out, I think!'

Already some of the party were pretty merry.

Marjorie showed her disapproval.

Cherry was chatting away to the vet. He was laughing and telling the others about his interview with Jane. They all thought it very funny, and although we thought it hilarious at home, I was getting a little annoyed at it becoming a public joke. I said, 'It is all very well, but you had kept Cherry late for weeks, and Jane had every right to be suspicious.'

A rather "made-up woman" said, 'Oh, he's usually with me.'

The vet said, 'Cherry is very funny. She leaves notes like "You are very late, I am going in five minutes. Going . . . Gone!"'

After a little while we excused ourselves, pleading tiredness after a long drive, and escaped with relief.

The next morning at breakfast, I had just slid into my place, late as usual, when father lowered his paper.

'I was driving to the golf club, when "Smiler", the AA man, stopped me. He said, "Excuse me, sir, but is it your daughter who drives a red and silver MG sports car, a pretty young blonde girl, with a younger dark-haired girl with her?" I nodded.'

'Well, sir, I thought you should know, they went past me last Friday doing 70 mph!'

I looked quickly at Jo. She had blushed, and regarded father, looking very rebellious. Father had his steely look. When his blue eyes became almost grey, we all held our breath.

'It is a very dangerous thing to do. Seventy miles an hour is far too fast, especially for a beginner. Your sister was with you and you could easily have killed both of you. A car is a lethal weapon. Remember my words, and I forbid you to drive over thirty mph, unless I am with you!'

After breakfast I went to Jo's room. She was furious.

'That deceitful "Smiler". I shall never wave at him again.'

'I agree.'

'He is a sneak, Why didn't he stop us, and give us a warning, instead of telling Daddy?'

'Don't worry, Jo, Daddy will soon forget. Driving at thirty in a sports car is just silly!'

The replies for the party were nearly all in, and excitement was mounting. Every morning it was discussed, much to Father's dismay. In exasperation he put down his *Times* and said. 'Are we still discussing this party? For goodness sake give it a rest, I am sick and tired of hearing about it!' He retired behind his paper. I got the giggles, and Jane gave me a warning look. We finished breakfast in silence.

It was the day of the dance. The house bustled with activity. The caterers arrived with their van, and set up chairs and little tables in the dining-room, pushing the great table to the side to take the buffet. Fuller and Jane arranged all the flowers, and it all

Jo

looked very festive. The party was timed for 9 pm and one by one
we came down in our finery. Father had on his white tie and tails,
and looked very handsome. He was checking the drinks with the
waiter. 'I do not want any one to be drunk. If you notice someone
getting intoxicated, just weaken their drink, or say it has run out.
It is better than trouble.'

    The little band was tuning up, and I was highly excited. I loved
to dance, and made a few requests for my favourite tunes.
Remembering to ask for Jo's special "Ain't Misbehavin'" and
"Love for Sale". After a slow start everyone seemed to arrive at
once. The evening passed in a blur of faces, voices, and sore feet!
Those heels were killing me! I saw Jo go into the conservatory with
Larry, and noticed Sally, the third member of the trio, they often
went out together, looking worried. I caught a glimpse of Jo
dashing upstairs, and Larry returned to Sally looking serious. I

slipped upstairs and found Jo sitting at the dressing-table. She was quite still, and large tears were slowly running down her cheeks.

'Jo darling, what's happened?'

She looked at me in the looking-glass, 'Larry has just told me he is going to marry Sally. I thought I was the one he loved!'

I was struck dumb, and just put my arms around her.

'Don't let them see you care. Dry your eyes, Daddy is just about to toast Marjorie and Jane. Come down and face it out or people will ask questions.'

Bravely she repaired her make-up, and we went down together. Luckily father was toasting Marjorie, and all attention was on her. The champagne was flowing, and I saw Jo dancing with Bill, another boy friend, who adored her, but sadly she had no feelings in return. Larry left with his new fiancée, which I thought showed some common sense. As the evening was drawing to a close, I noticed a radiant Marjorie disappear into the conservatory with Leo. I thought, I hope she is luckier than Jo! I was taken to dance by a friend, and never saw them emerge. The band played "God Save the King" and everyone went home.

I went to my room to undress, kicking off my shoes with relief. Just as I was putting on my dressing-gown, Cherry came in.

'Marjorie is in floods of tears, I don't know why. They are both crying, and won't say what is the matter! do you think you could help? They might tell you.'

I went into their room, and went up to Jo, 'What is the matter with Marjorie?'

Between sobs, Jo said, 'Leo is going back to his wife, his stepfather has threatened to disinherit him if he divorces his wife!' I just disappeared. Alone in my bedroom I thought if this is what it is like to fall in love, I want none of it!

5

The Stories of the First World War

The new term was due to start early the next week. As there was an atmosphere of deep gloom in Shawfield House, I was quite glad. At breakfast I announced the fact. Jo looked at me mournfully, and Marjorie said rather tartly, 'At least we shall have some peace.'

Father looked up from his paper, 'How about coming to the RAF Club for lunch on Saturday?' I accepted with pleasure. I enjoyed lunching alone with Father in lavish surroundings and I also knew that I would have another opportunity to find out more about his interesting past. He never failed to answer my questions and I was slowly beginning to understand him as a person. As his daughter to gain such insight into a parent's past and I felt strangely honoured.

It was my first visit to the Club on my own, and I was taken in at the side door in Park Lane, the Ladies' entrance, and we went through a narrow hall to the main staircase, which was lined with portraits of famous airmen. The large ante-room and bar were on the first floor, and we sat on a sofa while the barman took the order. Very few people were there, and it was easy to converse.

'Did you join the Club after the war, Daddy?'

'Yes, a group of young officers, including the Duke of York, got together, and the building was given to them, and the Club was formed.

'How did you get into the Air Force?'

'I started off in the Artists' Rifles, but I did not think foot-slogging was much fun, and as the young pilots were dying like flies, the powers that be asked if any of us would like to volunteer for the Royal Flying Corps. I put my hand up very fast. We were sent on a course to Oxford, and that was when I realised that all the study I made on insurance laws was useful because I knew I had the ability to absorb the written word. To gain a commission we had to have a working knowledge of the engine of an aircraft! I learnt the whole book by heart, and obtained top marks, although if they had taken me to an engine and asked me about the various parts I should have been lost! I was commissioned and sent to Salisbury Plain. You were a few months old, and your mother joined me there. The hope was to build up her strength, but sadly she developed consumption, and went into a sanitorium near-by.'

We went through to lunch in the first floor dining-room overlooking Green Park. It was a lovely room, and we had a window table, and it was fun to see all the activity in the park while one ate. The food was very good English cooking, roast meats, and lovely puddings.

'Did you like the Flying Corps?'

Father smiled and stroked his chin. 'I suppose it was one of the happiest times of my life. I was suddenly without responsibility, mixing with some very fine fellows, mostly from public schools, with no idea of the struggle of earning one's living. Their average age was twenty, much younger than me, and crazy to fly. They knew their lifespan would be short; they were a reckless, Devil-may-care crowd. Every night was a party, and I made some friendships that have lasted to the present day.'

'What were the aeroplanes like?'

He laughed, 'Mostly wood and wire, with the very low-powered engine in the middle. In some of them, if a wind was blowing at 70 mph they would go backwards.'

'Gosh! how did they manage to manoeuvre them?'

'Mostly they didn't, they always tried to attack the enemy from a height, and zoom down. They had to fire with a rifle, and there were no parachutes.'

'They must have been brave.'

'They were. You have often seen the photograph on my mantlepiece of Major Billy Wells? Well, he was flying over the trenches in France, and was mortally wounded, and flew back to base, dying as he landed, in order to save his observer's life.'

'What about the man you call "Ak Ak?"'

"Ak Ak" was a typical young pilot, no fear, and a little mad! One night at a mess party on the plain, we had all had quite a few drinks, and Ak Ak, army language for A.A. Knight, which was his name, said "Come with me, Fred, we are going to a dance in

Captain A. A. Knight 1916

Warminster." We went to his hanger, and to my astonishment he
had managed to get a cow onto the wings, tied securely to the
struts! It was the mascot of 72 Squadron, and had its horns painted
in the Squadron's colours. Being very merry, we climbed into the
plane, and flew the short hop to the next airfield, missing the trees
by inches, Ak Ak had forgotten the extra weight would tax the
engine. The cow was mooing, and doing all manner of unpleasant
things on the wings. We landed, and unloaded the poor animal,
which was none the worse for the ride, and led it into the dance! It
caused quite an uproar, and we left it there to return by road the
next day.' We both laughed.

'Daddy, what a thing to do! I am surprised you are alive to tell
the tale. What happened?'

'As you might expect, an unholy row! We were both sent for by
the CO the next morning, and given a severe reprimand. I was
particularly blamed, being the older man, and I was very contrite,

Major Kenneth Dowding 1916

and because the CO had a good sense of humour, and disliked the CO of the camp we visited, we were both let off with a threat of dismissal if such behaviour was repeated!'

'It makes me very sad to think of all those wonderful people dying.'

'That, my darling, is war.'

'How did you get started again after the War?'

'It was a grim time, I had been recalled from the Middle East when your mother died in March, 1918. I remember sitting in the dusty offices on Holborn Viaduct, the furniture all shrouded in dust sheets, and wondering what we were going to do for money. I saw my tin box under the table, and pulled it out, inside I found my life insurance policy. I had a bright idea. I went to the bank, and they lent me a thousand pounds against it. I was in business. Edward Jerwood was still in France, he had been wounded twice, but always returned to the Royal Berkshires, the only officer in his regiment to live through the War! There was a jewel sale coming on at Christie's the next week. I had marked an important diamond collet necklace. I reckoned it would fetch £800 to £900 pounds. The bidding was brisk, slowing about £600. My excitement rose. I was going to get it. It developed into a duel

Captain Fred Ward 1916

between another dealer and myself. The bid was £950 against me. I raised my catalogue at the last minute and it was knocked down to me at £1,000! As I was leaving the rival dealer stopped me on the stairs. "Young man, you have paid too much for that necklace."

"I do not agree, sir"

"I will give you 5% profit.'

"Sorry to disappoint you, sir, but it is worth much more."

The man grew red in the face, "Do you know who I am?"

"I am afraid not".

"Here is my card, come and see me in the office to-morrow."

He departed in a Rolls Royce."

'Who was he?'

'The card read "Adolf Weil" with an address in Hatton Garden. I went to his office the next day, and succeeded in selling him the necklace for £1,500! Not only that, but it started a life-time's friendship, with his offer to finance any deal I thought worthwhile, if he could have a half share of the profit. I was on my way!'

Once again I had persuaded father to delve into his past. The comparison between his earliest days and the success he was beginning to enjoy after the war fascinated me. He had always been a clever and brave man, never afraid to take risks. They were now paying off.

A rather jolly man came up to the table. 'Hallo Freddie, who is this young woman?'

'Hallo Jimmy. This is Mitzi, my youngest daughter. This is Jimmy Lawson.'

'Good Grief! I remember bouncing you on my knee on Salisbury Plain.'

We all laughed, and they chatted together. I thought what a difference from that stunning man in the photograph. He was now middle-aged with half spectacles, thinning hair, and rather round, but great fun.

It was time to leave, and in the taxi father said, 'I have decided to take Jo to Madeira with Jane in March. I have booked the sailing, and we are to stay at Reid's Hotel. I hope it will take her out of herself. She has taken that blow very badly.'

'Yes, I think you are right, it is Yolande's influence.' (Yolande was a French girl who stayed with us to learn English, and she and Jo became great friends.)

'She always told Jo to be serious with men!'

Father said, 'H'm.'

'Jo told me she did not want to live if she could not have him. Do you think she meant it?'

'I hope not, we shall have to see what Madeira can do. Marjorie is a different kettle of fish. She thinks I don't know, but I see Leo on Bromley platform when our train comes in. She is still seeing him!'

'Oh dear, it is a mess, I hope she won't get hurt again.'

We arrived at Victoria Station, and boarded the train.

The following Tuesday I returned to Farringtons. On our first night inspection by Matron she said, 'How did you get those two black toenails on your big toes?'

'I was dancing in high heels.'

'Serve you right!' and with a flurry of white starch she was gone.

I was now very happy at school; we were blessed with a very good group of teachers. They found that I was quite good at dramatics, and Miss Davies asked if I could have elocution, so that

Captain James Lawson 1916

I could learn to speak clearly, and project my voice.

The elocution mistress was a Miss Bourne, from Brook Green in London, a tiny creature, very old-fashioned, with faded red hair pinned on top of her head. She would stand in what she described as "Position one" with her strange pointed shoes at right angles.

'Now girls, deep breaths and slowly out.'

At first I was shaking with giggles, but managed to control them, and found she really did know her subject. We got along very well, and I was even invited to her Victorian house in the holidays.

At the end of term I returned home to find the family back from Madeira, with all kinds of presents, and some wonderful *chaises longues* for the garden. Jo seemed brighter, looked marvellous with her tan, but I often found her in tears.

One morning at breakfast Father looked up from his paper, folding it, he handed it to Marjorie, and said, 'What do you make of that?'

She went quite white. I thought she was going to faint. She gave the paper back to Father, and said, 'That appears to be that!' and

Ward Sisters, Cherry, centre back. Front left Jo, centre, Mitzi, right, Marjorie

left the breakfast table.

Jane said, 'What is it Fred?'

'That scoundrel Leo has just been made a father!'

It was hard for me to grasp the full significance of the news, but from the general reaction I realized it was very bad indeed.

Jane was worried about Jo, and insisted Dr Rogers, our GP whom we all adored, should come and give her a check up.

After the X-rays he found she had tuberculosis of the left lung. It was suggested that the East coast would be a good bracing place, and Jane went off in the car to find a suitable place for her to stay. She was there for several months, but was very unhappy at Clacton, and begged to be allowed to return home. They glazed the balcony outside Jane's bedroom and put her bed there.

They found her other lung was now affected. Dr Rogers said she had about six months to live.

During her illness she realized what a fine person Jane really was, after years of mistrust. It was mainly because I realised that my sisters had such poor opinion of me, that I pleaded with Jane to let me go to boarding school. I reasoned that if I removed

The Ward Brothers with their Mother 1916. Back row from the left, Edward, William, Walter, Fred. Front row from left, Arthur, Charlotte Ward and Albert.

myself from the family circle, they would then see I was no threat to them.

It was all because of Mama dying when I was eighteen months old; Jane was really my Aunt Annie, Mama's eldest sister. It was my idea to call her "Jane".

Father found himself with four of us under ten, and Mama had said to him, 'If you don't promise me that Annie will look after my children, I shall haunt you!' There was no other solution. Naturally after a few years, tongues started to wag, and father thought that as it was now legal to marry one's sister-in-law, that was the solution. They married on the thirtieth of June, 1919.

It was a very wet day, and although I was only two and a half, one of my most vivid memories is the misery of grandfather's back as he looked out of the window with the tears of rain running down the glass.

He deeply disapproved of the marriage, and so did Auntie Eva, the youngest sister.

The Ward Brothers, 1943. From left to right, Albert, Arthur, William, Edward, Walter and Fred

So from that day on there were two camps: Auntie Eva and my sisters, and Jane and me! So it was a heart-warming feeling for me now to have Jo's confidence and growing affection.

Jane was always at her call, and nursed her with great tenderness. Jo said to me, 'I know now who really loves me, and I think I was silly to want to die. Do you think I shall recover?'

I grinned and said, 'Of course you will, we are going to have a great time together. I am nearly fifteen, and the older I get the closer we shall become. We shall have to plan a wonderful holiday, for when you are stronger!'

Her face lit up. 'That would be fun, will you bring in some travel brochures?'

'Of course. I am going to Bromley tomorrow I shall have a search.'

'I should like a West Highland terrier. Do you think Daddy would let me have one?'

'Of course he would, I shall ask him.'

Sadly, it was impossible to find a West Highland puppy at short notice, but we bought a black Labrador puppy, which she adored.

6

Death in the Family

With so much on my mind of deep concern at home, I was ashamed to find that I could become so absorbed with my life and work at school that I would not give them a thought until I went to bed, or received a letter from home.

I returned after six weeks for a "Saturday break", and found some family friends at home, John and Mary Vaughan. John was a close business colleague of Father's and the conversation was about a trip they made together in 1919 to Austria. Father was explaining to Mary what had occurred.

I knew Father to be an excellent raconteur and quickly settled down, eager to listen.

'John and I arrived in Vienna on a very wet night, and took a cab to an address given to us by a Swedish jeweller, who owned an apartment in the city. We rang the bell, and the door was opened by the most beautiful blonde, in a white chiffon nightdress!'

I said, 'This is hospitality indeed!'

The woman laughed and said, 'Olaf said you would be coming, but not when. Do come in.'

Mary said, 'I suppose it was a bordello, Fred!' in her deep voice with a Knightsbridge accent.

'No it was not. Lisa was a charming woman, and showed us to our rooms, then donned a housecoat and made us a little supper. It was a large apartment, and we were very comfortable. The next day we put an advertisement in the equivalent to the Viennese 'Daily Mail', taking a double page and announcing our wish to purchase jewellery at good prices. The currency was falling fast, and people were desperate to get some money before it fell any further.'

John said, 'We took a suite at the Imperial Hotel. There were flunkeys on the doors, and they would bow from the waist every time we went in and out! We did enormous business, and Fred was pleading with the ladies not to sell everything, but save some against a total fall in the money.'

'Yes, I remember a very charming old lady, and I pleaded with her just to sell half, but she insisted that she would never be offered so much money again, and sold it all.

'We returned with the treasure in a Gladstone bag, so that it was easy for customs. At the German border we ran into trouble. They said our papers were not in order. So we were hauled off the train with our luggage.

'It was a sleepy little border town called Passau, and the Mayor was told two very important Englishmen had to be entertained, until their documents were confirmed by Vienna. The Mayor ordered a long table to be put in the square, and summoned the town band. It was a wonderful party with Austrian wine, and we were both fêted like royalty. The Mayor said, "We shall play your National Anthem." This rather put out the band, who could only produce "And her golden hair was hanging down her back!" So John and I stood to attention, and tried to keep straight faces. After that everyone unwound, and we had a good meal.

'The news came through that we could leave on the next train, but had to let the German border guard hold the bag of jewellery, right through Germany, leaving us at the Dutch border. We went in merry procession to the train, the band playing, with promises to return . . . The German guard was very fat, and sat between us, holding the bag of jewels.'

I looked at John, his face was alive with amusement. He was normally rather sinister in a good-looking way, a real ladies' man, very well-dressed, always had a red carnation in his button hole, and wore a navy blue overcoat with a velvet collar, lined with mink, which impressed me very much!

When he was killed in the war by the bombing, eight women including his wife, placed obituaries in *The Times!*

'Tell them, Fred, about the German wanting to go to the lavatory!'

'Well that was very funny. He said to me, "Please I want to be excused, will you hold the bag?"

We said, "No, it is to be in your hands right through Germany, one of us will come with you, but we cannot have the bag." So this performance went on through Germany.

When we arrived at the Dutch border the fellow was asleep, and did not realise it. When the train stopped at Amsterdam, we woke him up. He was very cross. We left him explaining to the Dutch!'

Jane said, 'Oh Fred, what a mean thing to do.'

'Not really,' said John, 'We had lost a day's business through the Germans being officious.'

'May we go and see Jo?'

'Yes Mary, she should be awake now. Does John want to come upstairs?'.

When they came down, John was distraught, striding up and down the drawing-room.

'Can't we do something, Fred? If it is money, I will gladly pay for the finest in the land.'

'Sadly, John, we have had the best, and they had her in the Brompton Hospital, and she had gold injections, but nothing has stopped the spread of the disease.'

'It's a bloody shame. I do not know how you can bear it.'

'There is no choice.'

Tea was brought in, and John was pleased to see Jane had given him his favourite jam tarts.'

They stood up to leave. Mary was going to visit an old lady in Chislehurst and Jane asked if they would drop me off at Farringtons. I dashed upstairs to Jo on the balcony. She was looking rather tired after all her visitors.

'Must go now, see you in three weeks. John and Mary are giving me a lift, back to Farringtons, it will save Jane turning out.'

We embraced and I raced downstairs.

John had a wonderful Lagonda, and we dropped Mary on the way, and I swept up to the doorway of West House, very impressive for all those little eyes peering from the window.

John kissed me goodbye, 'Be good if you can, if not, come to me!'

Inside the girls clustered round, 'Who was that?'

'Oh just a boy friend,' I said airily, with a broad grin.

There was a pageant at school of "Women in Literature through the Ages". Our headmistress, Miss Davies, took it all very seriously, and the press were invited for a photo-call; we were told to be dignified, not to speak of it as a show, but a pageant. I had been cast as Oliver Goldsmith's mother, for which I had to learn a southern Irish accent. I did not really like the part, and would have preferred something with meat, like Becky Sharp. So it was astonishing to me, when a photograph appeared in *The Daily Mirror* of me lying on my tummy on the front lawn, in a green poke bonnet, with my hands under my chin, and a broad grin! The caption read "One of the girls at Farringtons School, where they are holding a pageant of "Women of England" for their Founder's day on June 30th.

I was rather in disgrace with Miss Davies, but she soon forgave me. She would look over her half spectacles at meal times, and give me an indulgent smile.

'I hear you are a great mimic.'

It was my turn to blush, as she was one of my best subjects. We all had a week of sitting at "High", which was her table.

One morning I was sitting beside her and Babara Corrie, a Scots girl, was opposite me. She had very red cheeks in a long sheep-like face, and we were all dressed in our beige blouses and dark green tunics.

ONE OF THE GIRLS of Farringtons School, Chislehurst, who will be in the "Pageant of Schools and Scholars" on Foundations Day.

Mitzi in Pageant as Oliver Goldsmith's Mother

In true Scottish fashion Barbara sliced the top off her egg. It was a little soft, and went straight down the front of her tunic! Miss Davies turned to me and said, 'What is your opinion on The League of Nations? It killed my giggles stone dead, and I went into a complete fabrication of reasons why I thought it would save the world from war, all the time watching Barbara pulling her napkin down over the ghastly mess of egg out of the corner of my eye. When I thought she had cleaned up, I concluded my idiotic speech. Miss Davies smiled sweetly, 'I should like you to write me a paper on the British mandate in Palestine.' I nodded, and promised I would do some research, and put it on her desk by the weekend.

I returned home at the end of July, it was a wonderful Summer, and most days Fuller, the gardener, would carry the sad little frame of Jo down to the garden, under the copper-beech, so that she would be cool. She was now only weighing six stone, and her large brown eyes seemed to make up her whole face. Her lovely dimples had gone, and she looked ghastly.

Father was having business problems. The New York crash, which was followed by the French one, was now affecting London. Some New York dealers said they would give some jewels against their great debt. He arranged to take the German *Europa* to New York, spend the day there, and return on the same ship as she

Farringtons 1931, Miss Davies in centre Mitzi, end of front row on the right

turned around. He was so afraid Jo would die while he was away. He discovered upon arrival in New York that even those with money were refusing to pay, and would only offer "goods" against their debt. As all items of jewellery were only fetching 10 cents on the dollar of their previous to crash prices, it was not much help. He threatened to sue, but the reply was, 'Try it, we shall move to the next state!'

Allie Osterwald was very down-hearted, but agreed to work with father to try to salvage something from the wreck. Allie had had to sell his lovely home called Dream Acres. Sailing home, father wondered whether Shawfield House would have to go too.

We had fixed up our summer holiday in Jersey. We had never been there before. We had arranged it for the first fortnight in September, being certain things would have resolved themselves by then. It was not so, and we left London on the hottest day of the year, 90°, by train to Southampton, leaving Jane with Jo, with instructions from father to telephone at once if things worsened. None of us wanted to go, but it was argued that Jo would realise if we cancelled our holiday. We had only been there three days when we were asked to return at once.

She died on the thirteenth of September. The whole family fell apart, I seemed to be the only one who could cope. There were countless telephone calls to answer, and about a hundred letters, seventy wreaths came for the funeral, which was a real *Pompe Funèbre*. Two days after she died, Jane sent me to father's dressing-room for some aspirin. I had no idea father was home. He was sitting on his bed with a revolver in his hands.

'How DARE you enter my room without knocking?' He was as angry as I had ever seen him, but seeing the revolver in his hands, I knew I must brave it out.

'I am sorry, Daddy, I had no idea you were in. I was sent for some aspirins. What are you doing with the gun?

'If you must know, I was trying to screw up enough courage to kill myself! I have been ruined in the City. The banks have foreclosed on my credit, I owe £150,000 in three City banks, and I have no way of paying.'

I put my arms round him. 'Please, Daddy, don't use the gun. You know you have the heart of a lion. We shall do all that we can, it is all these dreadful things coming together, I do understand. We shall need you to help us all.'

'I think you were sent at the exact minute as my guardian angel, although I could have wished for a prettier one!' We both laughed.

'Can I get you a brandy?'

'That's a good idea!'

I realised with terror in my heart it was still in the bedroom where Jo was lying in her coffin. I would not admit my fear, so I went in and steeled myself to look at her lying there. Wrapped in white lace with flowers, she looked beautiful, my fear went, and I thought what a waste, she had so much to give, and it is just thrown away. I grabbed the bottle of brandy, and returned to father. I promised him to keep the little episode as our secret.

We were all taken to the local dress shop and fitted out in black for the funeral. It was still perfect weather on the day of the funeral. Edward Jerwood arrived to help us all, and we stood in the morning-room while the coffin was carried down the stairs. Uncle Jerwood helped us by his calm dignity, and we all went out to take our place in the cortège of eight black limousines, to go in procession to the service in Bromley Parish Church. The coffin went before us laden with flowers. The undertakers walked from the outskirts of Bromley. Being Saturday, the town was crowded. People stopped and bowed their heads. It seemed so unreal, like a bad dream. In church I had difficulty in holding back the tears when a woman sang "I know that my Redeemer liveth" but I clenched my hands and held on because I knew that once the tears started I should be unable to stop.

I was allowed to return to the house, I just could not face the burial. I knew now that childhood was behind me. One had to face the future, which had all the indications of not being very rosy . . .

I returned to school after the weekend. Matron was watching as I unpacked and she noticed my black dress. 'A black dress at your age?'

I was embarrassed because I knew that she would be by my reply. 'It was for my sister's funeral last Saturday.'

'I am sorry,' she said and quickly left the room.

During the term I thought deeply about ways and means to help in the family crisis. There was no way that I could matriculate with my lack of arithmetic. I tried very hard to improve, but often took my long division over three pages, and I was always getting "returned lessons", which meant one had to take the exercise book to Miss Davies, and show her how idiotic one was in that subject. Strangely I was top at Latin and French, and History was my great subject. Miss Davies shook her head sadly. 'You are not unintelligent but somehow your mind cannot cope with arithmetic. I wonder why that has happened?'

'I think it was the mistress at day-school, she always pulled my pigtails if I had nothing written down, so I did not try to reason things out, I just wrote anything!'

Miss Davies was rather shocked. 'That was a stupid thing to do, no wonder your mind goes blank now!' She gave her gentle laugh, slightly rocking as she did so.

It crystallized my thoughts and I resolved to speak to father at my first opportunity.

My chance came during the holidays, we were lunching at "Kettners". The very expensive restaurants were now finished for us but I always loved this restaurant. I told father of my conversation with Miss Davies, and asked him if I could leave school in the Spring term. He looked at me very seriously. 'You are only just sixteen, you will not be properly educated. Do you not think that is unwise?'

'Well, Daddy, I shall never matriculate, and therefore never be able to go on to college. It seems to me, that with my schooling costing you hundreds of pounds a term that you can ill afford, it would be wiser to let me leave, and study to go on the stage.' He drew himself up in his chair.

'Let us get one thing straight. I may let you leave school, but you are NOT going to become an actress. I know the pitfalls of that profession, and I have had quite enough trouble with my other daughters, without you going head long into disaster.'

I just grinned. Somehow I would find a way.

As it was our first Christmas without Jo, it was decided to spend the holiday at an hotel in Bournemouth. Marjorie and Cherry were quite excited at the idea. We arrived at the hotel, and that night at dinner father ordered his usual bottle of wine. As Jane did not drink, I had very little, and neither of my sisters drank very much, it was ample to our requirements. I noticed a party of three sitting near us,

A rather large lady, a very pretty young woman, and a personable young man. We later met during the dance, they were the Marments from Ascot, Mrs Marment was boasting about Phyllis, her daughter, being friends with the famous débutantes of the year, and Charles, her son, was socially in great demand. He said to Father, 'You don't believe in giving your daughters much to drink. We were very amused at the one bottle of wine!'

Father's eyes glinted, he smiled and said, 'They always have as much as they require.'

I thought that was rather rude, perhaps it was his sense of humour. Over the holiday, Marjorie and Charles became friends, and when we said our "Goodbyes" there were promises to meet soon.

My last term at school soon passed, I hated leaving, Miss Davies sent for me at the beginning of term, and I went to her comfortable study in East House.

'Come and sit down, dear. I have received a letter from your Father saying you wish to leave us at the end of term. You are very young, and still have much to learn, are you not happy here?'

'Miss Davies, I really do not want to leave, but my father has had a great set-back in business, no one has repaid their debts to him. He now has to repay three banks about £450,000, and it will mean a great struggle. He has promised to pay back every penny, and the banks have agreed, taking the deeds of our house and his life insurance as security. They do not want further cut-backs, as they wish to keep his image as a strong merchant. There are hardships for my parents, with most of the staff leaving, and the great house to run. I do not want to indulge myself at his expense. I am not clever enough to matriculate, and I think I should leave and try to earn my living. I should like to be an actress but father

*Marjorie's wedding,
September 1934. (Charles,
Marjorie Marment and
Eve Young*

is against it.'

'That is a pity, as you have considerable talent in that field.'

'Would you tell him that? It might help.'

In fact, she wrote a letter, but it was no good; father would not be persuaded.

I was sent to a Miss Gooding, for tuition in shorthand and typing. She was far too easy-going, and I never really learnt properly, and my heart was not in it. Gladys Hatherill was to be married, so there was a vacancy in the office. Jim Trehearne, Father's junior partner, was to take over the books, and I was to do the typing and learn to string pearls. I hated it! This was not what life was about for me, each day to London, sitting at a desk, poking pearls about with a needle. It was very tedious, to say the least. I applied to the Beckenham Amateur Dramatic Society, and to my delight was accepted, and given two parts at once. It was a splendid diversion, and I learnt very quickly. To father's horror my first part was a tart in a skit on Shakespeare by A A Milne. I had to wear a blonde wig, and the consternation of father's face when I walked into the drawing-room with it on was hilarious.

'What have you done to your hair?'

'Don't be silly, Daddy, it's only a wig!'

We had visited the Marments of Ascot. It turned out to be a small provision shop in the high street, and the family lived over it!' father was very put out, and Jane was most indignant.

'All that chat about débutantes! Rubbish!'

By now Marjorie was on a big rebound from Leo, and Charles Marment seemed very keen. I am afraid our auras never mixed. I found him too possessive, and very jealous. Father said, 'Don't rock the boat. She has to make up her own mind.'

Jane said, 'You should start as you mean to go on. If he annoys you, tell him.'

They became engaged in January and Marjorie was so happy, one had not the heart to spoil it for her. I just tried to keep out of the way.

Father said to Jane, 'Have we got him for life?'

Jane laughed, 'If the marriage takes place, I am afraid you have!'

They were married the following September, and that was the end of our close relationship with Marjorie.

7

I work in London

Life was beginning to become much more interesting, and I was getting to terms with my work, making my fun in the people I met in the course of the day. I now had the policeman on point duty at Holborn Circus taped. Every morning, when he saw me coming, he would hold up the traffic so that I could cross quickly, and not be late. I paid my week's lunch money to Marie, in Fetter Lane. She was the wife of a docker. Her café was simple fare and cheap. A shilling was the cost of lunch and one was able to have meat and two vegetables and a sweet. My salary was twenty-five shillings a week. I told father it was slave-labour. He grinned and said, 'You do very well, you do not pay for your lodging, or food'. I was rather miffed at the idea that he could even think I should!

I was sitting at my table working on an enormous bunch of pearls from India with silver bindings round about forty strands of pearls, each one having a silver tassel. My work was to grade them into necklaces, sorting out the various colours, so that one had matching pearl necklaces. Being natural pearls, they came in a variety of colours. Dark pearls with an orange tinge were supposed to be favoured by the darker skinned women of South America, while the *crème rosée* were suitable for English skins. Father came through from the office.

'I have just heard that the Sheik of Bahrain is coming with his sons. He is interested to see how we handle the pearls.

'Are they coming to my table?'

'Yes, I want to show them how you work.'

They arrived, all in flowing burnouses, not at all like my memories of Rudolph Valentino! They had hard faces, with rather hooked noses, and piercing black eyes. I went on calmly picking up pearls with my tongs, and answered their questions as politely as I

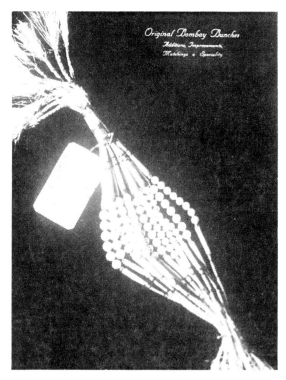

Pearl Bunch 1936

could. I must admit they scared me a little, they looked so uncompromising, with no gentleness in their faces. To my relief they finally went into the front office. Father came through again after they left. He was rocking with laughter.

'Why are you laughing, Daddy?'

'I have just had a marvellous offer of carpets and camels in exchange for you, as a bride, for his son!'

The rest of the office collapsed in hysterical laughter. I joined in, but I was alarmed. Father never refused a good offer!

'What did you say?'

'I thanked him very kindly, and said I appreciated the honour, but you were already betrothed.'

I really did laugh that time. However, I took the precaution of going home a different way, just in case they had any ideas of kidnapping!

I noticed to my secret delight that I was beginning to be attractive to the opposite sex.

In the thirties we were incredibly innocent. Sex was never

discussed, and it was quite taboo to sleep with anyone before marriage. Jane said that it was only done by servants or débutantes. And God help this country when the middle class lost its standards! Like all young women I liked to play with fire, and lead a man as far as I dared, then make a run for safety. Names of dangerous escorts were quickly exchanged between me and my friends, and they were struck off invitation lists! I noticed that quite benign-looking young men in glasses were often very passionate, and I learnt to run when they removed their spectacles! My friends and I all wanted to know what the future held. My friend Maisie, who worked with me in the office as secretary, told me that there was an Indian selling perfume in "Wallis's" at Holborn Circus who would tell one's future for the price of a bottle of scent. At the lunch hour we scuttled up Hatton Garden, and searched through the large store for the "Mystic Man of the East".

He was a rather fat lugubrious gentleman in a gold and red turban. He looked at my hand, and shook his head sadly. 'You will not marry until late in life, then it will be to an artist, and you will have no children.' I was rather embarrassed, and thanked him, giving him his shilling, and left with Maisie doubled up with laughter. I was rather disappointed. It did not sound very exciting, when one was nineteen. Maisie said, 'I can just see you as an artist's model in Chelsea!' I thought, what can one expect for a shilling? and dismissed it from my mind.

The next morning I answered a ring at the office door, looking through the little trap door I saw a beautiful blonde woman.

'May I see Mr Ward?'

'May I ask your name?'

'Madame Margolow.'

I invited her into the corner office. She walked before me, beautifully dressed in navy and white, with attractive gold jewellery. She had the appearance of a good buyer! I went into the front office. Father seated at his desk, bent over an emerald, which he was studying with his loupe. Jim Trehearne, his partner, was sitting in the other corner working on the accounts. Father looked up, 'A Madame Margolow to see you,' I said with a broad grin. His face was a study of consternation and panic!

'Where is she?'

'In the corner office.'

'Right, tell her I shall be with her in one minute.'

After she left, Father came through to my office. He bent over me and whispered, 'Not a word about this at home. Have lunch with me on Saturday.' I nodded agreement.

Father's reaction to the mysterious visitor's arrival made me think that this time I would learn something about his past personal life. I knew how he had achieved success in the business world, but he had been reticent about more intimate matters.

We went to the club and when we were sitting in the great ante-room having our drinks, he said, 'I want to explain to you who the visitor was who came to the office last Thursday. There would be great trouble at home if Jane learnt of her visit. Many years ago, I met this lady in Vienna, and fell in love. We arranged to meet in the South of France the next Spring and it was an experience I shall treasure all my life. I wanted to marry her, but when I wrote to Jane asking for my freedom, she refused.

(Pictures flashed across my mind of scenes in a boarding house in Bournemouth when we were all very young, of Jane standing in the bedroom with a letter in her hand. Auntie Eva was there, and Jane was in a fury!)

'Let him bring her to this country. I shall scratch her eyes out!')

'I am sorry, Daddy, I know Jane has always been very jealous. I suppose this was the root of it. I wonder why she would not free you'

'Jane thought no one else would look after you children like she could, especially a "foreigner" and of course her relatives backed her up in that.

Lisa and I decided the best solution was to say nothing, and meet for idyllic spells abroad. However time really does even things out, and now when we meet it is as dear friends. Naturally Jane knows nothing of this, although I think she has her suspicions. I tried to make it up to her by having our child, but as you may remember, he was stillborn, and it nearly killed her.'

'Yes Daddy, I remember the straw outside the house in Bromley High Street, to deaden the noise of the buses when she was so very ill, and Nurse Waltzden who would take me for walks in the afternoon.'

'Let us go and have a good lunch, and dismiss these sad thoughts.'

'Daddy do you think I could call you "Freddie" from now on? We are real friends, and I feel so silly in the office calling you "Daddy" in front of strangers!'

Amusement spread over his face, and he put back his head and roared with laughter. 'That's a great idea, I should like that, we shall have a good bottle of wine to celebrate!' It caused a little consternation at home, but they soon became used to my calling him "Freddie".

Strangely the "Mystic Man of the East" who foretold an artist in my life, proved to be a true visionary, and I shall tell of the artist's life, running parallel with mine, as I write the rest of my story. His name, Charles McCall.

8

Edinburgh

Charles McCall trudged up the Mound in Edinburgh. It was with a light heart as he had heard that morning that he was to be admitted as a full-time student to the Edinburgh College of Art. For years he had attended the night classes of "Life" drawing. It had been the only thing that brought him alive. Studying under D M Sutherland, an encouraging and brilliant teacher who, knowing of Charles' home difficulties, gave him every aid that was possible, feeling a kinship with Charles' mother's Caithness origins, which matched his own. He was a delightful raconteur, and would tell the class humorous and colourful stories of his life in the highlands. A great friendship had grown between D M, as he was known to the students, and Charles, and he had persuaded and encouraged him to enter for the scholarship to the College. The prize was his and at last he could pack away all the dreary jobs he had had to do in order to live. His home life was difficult. His two elder brothers had been smitten by meningitis when they were two and three years old, leaving his mother with a great burden on her shoulders, and making his father an embittered man. William McCall, his father, had a remarkable bass voice, and was invited to go to Milan to study, but sadly, through his troubles, he had to refuse, but sang in the choir at St Giles' Cathedral.

When Charles first realised he had a talent in drawing, he begged to be allowed to study art.

'No it is too risky,' he was told. So he was apprenticed to a very wealthy lawyer who was a hard man, and paid eight shillings a week. Charles was allowed no mistakes, and if his nose ran while he was taking dictation, he was forbidden to blow it. The interesting thing about this man was that when he heard that Charles had success with his drawing, he went to his father and offered to put

Charles Sketching 1934

up the money for the College. It was refused, as his father thought he would never make a living in art. So there were other jobs, one as a manager in a toffee factory in Dundee . . . but always the art classes at night.

Now today his chance had come! He straightened up his thin shoulders as he entered the College door. This was the start of living.

His drawing improved by leaps and bounds under D M's expert tuition. Full-time study made such a difference. He was being taught painting by David Foggie, who was very pleased with his efforts, and to his joy won the Royal Scottish Academy travelling Scholarship in 1933. At last he could go back to Paris. Charles had four maiden aunts, a legacy from The First World War. His favourite was Aunt Liz, the eldest. She and Aunt Hannah ran a very successful ladies' underwear shop, and when he was twenty-one, she pushed twenty-one pounds into his hand, urging him to go

David Foggie (Teacher of Painting, Edinburgh College of Art)

to Paris. He felt a deep gratitude to Aunt Liz. It was not the first time she had come to the rescue, always quietly, with a finger on her lips. Her sisters were all so different, Aunt Jean, the next sister, was a seamstress at "Jenner's" and held a very good position there, but she had a very sharp tongue, and had to be handled with care. There were no hidden gifts from her, and anything that was given had to be received with due humility! The third sister, Aunt Hannah, worked with Aunt Liz, and was a good businesswoman, quite different in appearance from the other three sisters, who were blonde with blue eyes, and very attractive when young. Hannah favoured the Smith side of the family, very dark, with strong striking features, and a dry sense of humour. The youngest of the four women was "Belle", very excitable, talkative, and she ran the house for the others. William McCall, being the only son in the family, was highly regarded by his sisters, but his poor wife caught all the criticism.

Nude Art Class — Charles McCall

Monsieur and Madame Dauchez — Paris 1937

Charles went to Paris for the first time in 1928. He never forgot his excitement at seeing the beauty of the city, the light, the French way of life. The Art Galleries fired his imagination, and strengthened his determination to become a painter. It opened his eyes to the possiblies of the future that could be his, if only he could complete his training. His grey eyes sparkled as he thought of the two years he was to spend in Europe, with the help of his scholarship.

Paris looked even better to him when he arrived. The French porters swarmed around him at the Gare du Nord, but he had no need of them, and went by Metro to the Boulevard St Michel, which was near his boarding house in rue d'Assas. He had been booked into the Pension Pinson, where most of the students from Edinburgh College of Art stayed. It was close to the Jardin du Luxembourg, and near the French Art Schools he was to attend.

He left the Pension early in the morning for his class in the *atelier* of André Lhote where he did some "Life" drawing, and in the afternoons would roam through Paris, sometimes sketching in the Luxembourg gardens. Quite often he would meet a heavily-built Frenchman on the stairs. He was bearded, with glasses and one morning they walked down together, 'Do you like Pension Pinson?'

'It is clean enough, but the food is rather meagre and dull.'

'May I ask how much you pay?'

Charles mentioned the sum.

'My name is Fernand Dauchez, I live on the next floor from the pension. Why do you not come and stay with us we will give you much better value for your money. Come and meet Madame Dauchez tonight.'

Charles was excited. To stay with a French family would be much more interesting, he could speak French, and improve his converstation. That night he went to the Dauchez's apartment. It was very comfortable middle class French and Madame Dauchez was a round little woman, obviously not as erudite as her husband, but very motherly.

'You are too thin, I will feed you like a turkey-cock for five shillings a day, everything included.'

It was quickly agreed, and Charles moved in the next day.

It was a great addition to his stay in Paris. He would discuss his work with Dauchez every evening, over a delicious meal provided by Madame Dauchez. They introduced him to their niece, Françoise, who had a good knowledge of painting, and took him to all the interesting exhibitions in the City. They soon became emotionally involved but, being a strict Catholic, Françoise would allow nothing more than kisses. The time came to return to Edinburgh for the next term, which he did with promises to come back on his next break.

Upon his return to college, he found he was to study painting under S J Peploe, a much-respected Scottish painter. It was a

Charles McCall. Graduation Day

very valuable experience. He found Peploe a shy man, who insinuated his meaning, never painting on one's canvas. He said that when he was young, he would chalk up on his studio wall "RELATIONS IN PLANES". At first McCall was mystified, and slowly it dawned on him what Peploe meant.

His joy was great the day Peploe stood behind him, 'That's it you've got it! You have absorbed what I have been saying, well done!'

A friendship grew between them, and they would discuss at length the problems of painting. Sadly, the heat of the classrooms and the work proved too much for Peploe's frail constitution and he died that year.

Charles won his diploma in 1934 with distinction, taking only two years against the normal four, and went on to Edinburgh University to study in the class of Professor David Talbot Rice, obtaining his First class Certificate of Merit 1934–1935, with high distinction.

With all his degrees secure he now relaxed. His painting of "Laura", which Peploe said was like a young Franz Hals, had been his diploma painting, and D M sent him down to London to be

William McCall 1936 (Charles McCall's father)

"mothered" by a painter friend of his called Nora Smith. She found him a studio in Redcliffe Road, which he rented. She was next door. If Nora had a model, Charles would go and paint in her studio to save money.

He received news from Edinburgh that he had won the Royal Scottish Academy Traveller for two years. He was elated. Now he could return to Paris and Françoise.

9

We were all very upset by the death of George V.

Particularly Freddie and Jane. A good friend of ours called Archie Graham was over from New York, and invited us to his hotel room to watch the Royal Funeral procession. I had never seen one before, and was not prepared to be so moved by all the solemn pomp and ceremony. I was rather excited because with the excuse of Royal mourning, I was allowed to buy a little black hat with an eye veil! We arrived early about 9 am, so that we could have access through the crowds. Archie Graham was an amusing man, rather like Mr Magoo in the cartoons, and he had with him, a large English man, who was introduced as "H G Wells", secretary. We all had coffee in the main hall, and it surprised me to see several ladies walk past us with great black veils covering their hats. Freddie thought they must be leaving for Westminster Abbey for the service. When it drew near to the time for the cortège to pass, we went to Archie's room to watch. It was all very dramatic, with the bands playing Chopin's "Funeral March". The hearse came into view, with the sailors pulling it up the hill. The Royal coffin looked so small with the Crown and Sceptre on the top, and one had a confused impression of deep purple, and Union Jacks. The King's four sons were all in Guards' uniforms, followed by all the foreign dignitaries. It was quite a long procession, and one was struck by the stillness of the crowd on the pavements, heads bowed in sorrow. We went down to the lounge when it was over, and had a snack lunch. Archie said, 'What do you think of the new King, Fred?'

'A good chap, a little too much to the left for the present Prime Minister, Mr Baldwin. He may have a hard time with him.'

'We hear strange reports in America about his affair with Mrs

Simpson!'

'It is very hushed up here, but of course the jewellery trade has been buzzing with rumours for months. I should think this sad event will finish it. We would never have her as Queen. She is divorced once, and is still married to Simpson.'

We all got ready to leave, and I put out my hand to Mr Shaw, the large man. He gave me his left hand, 'I cannot use my right hand I scratched it playing golf last week, and it is slightly infected.'

When I saw Archie Graham next in the office, he said, 'Remember the large man I brought to the funeral?'

'Of course. Nice chap.'

'He died three days later of poisoning from that small cut on his finger!'

The whole year was full of speculation about the king, reaching its climax on December 10th with the Abdication speech. We all sat in silence listening to the broadcast. Freddie's face was like stone. He was very upset. I was near to tears, and furious with Mrs Simpson for letting it happen. Jane was cross with the Prime Minister. 'Beastly old man. He could not stand him helping the miners, and saw it as a chance to get rid of him.'

Freddie was worried about the new king and his speech impediment. We all went to bed in a very sombre mood.

Once the Duke of Windsor had married Mrs Simpson, we put the business out of our minds. Much greater worries were on the horizon with the growing power of Adolf Hitler.

Freddie had bought a new car, and I wanted to learn to drive.

'I will teach you,' he said. However, I privately did not think he was very good at driving, it was always accompanied by 'Damn and blast' when he stalled the engine and his clutch and gear work seemed rather dodgy to me. So I went to our local garage, and paid £5 for six lessons.

Freddie was very cross. 'Waste of money! I could have taught you. Why pay?'

'Well, I have to pass a driving test, and I though they would know what the examiners require of one.'

The young man who came to instruct me was obviously very bored with the whole thing. He was very hard on me, made me learn to double-declutch, although our new car had the latest synchromesh gears.

'You may have to drive an old car some day and, what is more, take this book and learn how engines work.'

I struggled with backing and turning and when I made mistakes, sarcasm was poured on my efforts. If I had not had that perverse streak in me and wanted so desperately to drive, I would have given in; but I stuck it out.

At the end of my course of lessons my hated tutor said, 'I have fixed up for your examination on Saturday. It is in Lewisham and I shall drive you there, and wait while you are tested, because I do not think you will pass!'

I dressed very carefully, with a good pair of sheer silk stockings, Lanvin perfume, and with dreadful butterflies set out with my tutor for the test. The examiner was a nice middle-aged man, and he was amused at my names, Eloise Jerwood. I explained that I never used them now but was known as "Mitzi".

'I am Archibald!' We both laughed and I felt relaxed. We drove all through Lewisham, which had tram-lines, and I had to keep stopping for the people to get on and off the trams.

'I have never driven with trams before.'

'You are doing very well, I shall take that into account when I mark you.'

I had the usual stop on a steep hill, and three-point turn. All went well until I backed round a corner, and my foot slipped, and we shot round! I looked at "Archie" with dismay.

'To think I did it perfectly last night!'

I was showing a piece of thigh in my efforts. I thought he was amused. He asked me some very stiff questions, and I came out 10 out of 10. I was rather downhearted because I thought my backing would have ruined my chances. We returned to his office. We sat in the car while he added up the points. He turned to me with a beaming smile. 'You have passed, but you must promise me to practice backing round a corner.' I was elated, and thanked him very much.

'You did very well, or I would have failed you.

I went into the office for my instructor, purposefully looking very solemn. He rose to his feet looking very bored. 'Failed I suppose!' I laughed.

'No, I passed first time!' He was almost cross.

'Miracles do happen. Do you want to drive home?'

'No, I am too excited, I prefer you to drive.'

Freddie was delighted, and so was Jane, and I was immediately requisitioned to drive Papa to the golf club the next day!

Freddie came in the following evening in great excitement.

'I have booked up to take you and Jane to Paris for our Summer holiday. Cherry does not want to come, preferring to stay with her friends on the East Coast.'

'How wonderful! I have always wanted to go to Paris' I said.

Jane had mixed feelings because she always dreaded the Channel crossing!

William McCall 1934
(The artist's father)
40 x 25 ½"   Oil on Canvas
Private Collection   Charles McCall

Canal — Belgium
Drawing.   *Charles McCall*

Children Playing
Jardins du Luxemborg. Paris 1937.
Drawing courtesy of J.W. Keffer
Charles McCall

Head of Maxine
Private Collection 11 x 8" Oil on Board
Charles McCall

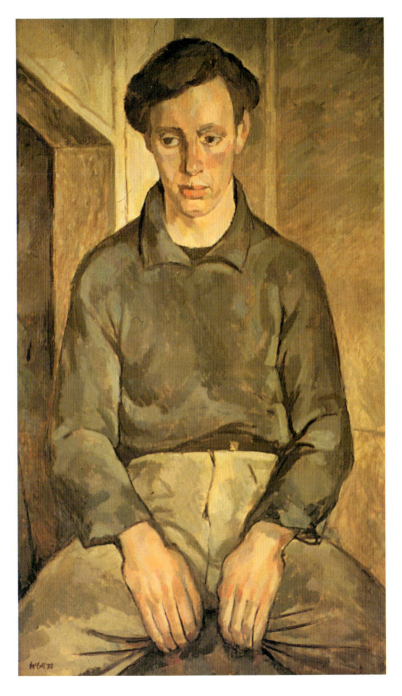

The Young Man
34 x 21" Oil on board.
Courtesy of J.W. Keffer
Charles McCall

The Black Forest — Germany
Drawing. *Charles McCall*

Sienna
Drawing.

Laura — the girl in the blue dress
18½ x 9"   Oil on board.   Charles McCall

10

Paris 1937

We left Bickley on a beautiful July evening. There was the usual fuss with Freddie always ready early, and Jane never ready on time! We drove to Newhaven, Freddie driving, with the usual damning and blasting when he stalled the car on hills.

I was bubbling with excitement, as we drove alongside the ship, we were crossing Newhaven — Dieppe, arriving in Dieppe at 5 am. Jane and I were in a cabin together, and Freddie in the male section. Poor Jane was quite green three miles from the port, and was put straight to bed by a motherly stewardess. The crossing was very smooth, and uneventful. It was fascinating to see the tall grey houses on the port, with the French officials in their peaked round caps, and swirling capes, bustling about. At once it was foreign, the smell of Gauloise and, not so pleasant, French urine!

After a great deal of shouting, the car was unloaded by crane, and we were on our way. We drove into Paris in the afternoon, a very nervous Freddie at the wheel, we were staying at the Plaza Athénée which was easy to find, being just off the Champs Elysées. It was very impressive, teaming with people to carry luggage, and rather lordly hall porters. The car was put away by the doorman, and we were taken to our rooms. I had a small room at the side of the hotel, and my parents had a large double room with bath on the front. We arranged to have a rest, and meet at 7.30 pm.

We had changed for dinner, and decided to go to the hotel bar to have a cocktail before leaving for the restaurant.

'I am going to give you your first champagne cocktail, to drink to our holiday!' Freddie was grinning, he was in party mood. I watched with fascination while the barman placed lumps of sugar in the glasses, poured brandy over them, adding the champagne, very chilled, finishing with a cherry on a stick. Jane watched us

77

Yolande Hartog (Lanvin)

with amusement, sipping her Perrier. It was wonderful, and my eyes began to sparkle, and Freddie was full of fun.

'That was delicious Freddie, a great treat!'

'Right, now we shall take a taxi to a restaurant I know in the Bois.'

The taxi-driver was frightfully cross-eyed, and Freddie said, 'I hope he knows where he's going, and not where he's looking!' This gave me the giggles, which inspired Freddie to make silly remarks all the way. We were soon at the restaurant, and had a table in the garden. It was magical. We had a carefully chosen meal, and returned home early, so that we should be fresh for the next day's events

Yolande Hartog, our friend of many years standing since she stayed with us to learn English, arrived early. There was much excitement and emotion. It was the first time we had met since Jo, her great friend, died. Yolande was small and very neat, dressed in

green cotton with white pique collar and cuffs, and a Breton sailor
hat in coarse black straw. She looked so chic that at once I felt
large and clumsy. She brought us all Lanvin perfume, and said
that she would be marrying Dr Michel Lanvin in the Spring of
next year, when he qualified, and would Freddie let me come for
the wedding? We all went out, and Freddie left us to go to his
office with Jo Templier in Rue Auber.

We went to a dress show at Lanvin's. The *Vendeuse* approached
and said, 'This dress is made for you!' It was an elegant evening-
dress in black, costing about £200, nearly my year's salary! It was
a great experience, and really ruined me for life in my taste for
dress.

I told Yolande that we were going to Longchamps for the Grand
Prix that afternoon. 'Let me come back with you and I shall tell
you what to wear.'

I thought my off-the-peg wardrobe did not impress her very
much! However, she selected a navy linen dress with a loose jacket
with white pique revers, and my white Breton sailor hat.

'Not bad' she said with her imperious French way. I had to
laugh.

'I do my best with the money I have'

'I know, eet is easy for me, Jeanne Lanvin insists that I wear her
clothes as I am to marry Michel.'

We went to Longchamps that afternoon and it was quite an
experience, with all the smart Parisiennes in wonderful creations.
Freddie had been tipped to back an Italian horse for the Grand
Prix. It was an exciting race. The French jockeys tried to box the
Italian horse in, but it suddenly broke through and won by a
length! Freddie was elated, and we returned to the hotel in high
spirits, his winnings paid for our stay at The Plaza Athénée.

I was shown all the sights, and made Jane go up the Eiffel
Tower with me. I think my most enjoyable visits were to
Napoleon's tomb, the top of the Arc de Triomphe and the great
star of avenues, and Notre Dame.

There was no doubt I was in love with Paris! Freddie thought a
visit to the Left Bank would amuse me, 'Le Quartier des Artistes''.
We sat in one of the large cafés on Boulevard Montparnasse. No
sooner had we sat down than an Arab came up to the table and
put a few monkey nuts down in front of me. This delighted
Freddie, it had happened at all the cafés, and I was always the one
to be given the nuts. 'They know who the monkey is!' said Freddie
laughing, and we all laughed. I noticed a tall good-looking

Mitzi 1937   *Charles 1937*

bearded man sitting opposite with a dark rather intense French girl. He was obviously amused by the little incident, but she just glanced at us and said, '*Je suis en retard, il faut partir, Charles.*'

So, I knew the name of the attractive man we had amused but I wasn't to know that he had reached a crisis in his life, nor that we would meet again years later in equally romantic but less peaceful circumstances. If I had then been a fly on the wall . . .

As they left the café Charles McCall thought about the little family of English tourists. They were so care-free; if only he could resolve his problems as easily. He turned to Françoise. 'Much as I hate decisions, I think I must face up to the great problem we share. You will not marry me unless I become Roman Catholic. That is impossible for me, with my Scottish upbringing, so I think the best thing I can do is to leave Paris, and continue my journeys.'

She was silent, but they both knew it was the end of their relationship.

We returned to Freddie's Paris office in Rue Auber. I was introduced to Georges Templier, a small delicate man of great charm, and to his daughter Denise, a pretty young girl of sixteen. Paul Marie was there. He worked for Georges, a strange character, very vain, full of *joie de vivre* and very excited to show Jane and me their suite of offices. We were shown lovely jewels, and a marvellous necklace of natural black pearls, the largest in size I had seen.

'Look Mitzi, see the lovely blue-green sheen, that is the best you will ever see. To be worth money, they must have that sheen, and be black. The minute there is a hint of brown, don't touch them!'

We left for our hotel with promises to meet Paul Marie with his wife at a restaurant later. Freddie had known Paul's father well in the twenties, and described him as a very fine man. Charles Marie had been very wealthy, but sadly inflation and the crash in 1930 had ruined the family fortune. When he died, Paul joined the firm of Jo Templier et fils, which we had just visited.

Between the wars, Freddie visited Paris every two weeks, often accompanied by Allie Osterwald from New York. Together they would set the place alight! There was no holding Allie when he was in party mood. One night, they had had a very good day's business, Allie invited everyone in the small restaurant to drink champagne with him, and bought a flower seller's basket, and gave flowers to all the ladies present, much to Freddie's amusement!

Now those days were gone, and every penny was hard fought over. With the coming of cultured pearls Freddie was very concerned about "real" oriental pearls, because it was almost impossible in the good cultured pearls to tell one from the other. Freddie started the Laboratory of the London Chamber of Commerce, for the Jewellery section. He employed two good scientists, Mr Anderson and Mr Payne. He and Anderson came to Paris and evolved the endoscope, which was basically a mirrored needle inserted into the pearl, reflecting a very strong light, showing the formation of the pearl. A real pearl, which is formed by a small piece of grit irritating an oyster, is covered by the oyster with layers of pearl, so that it shows up in X-ray like an onion. The cultured pearl is a mother-of-pearl bead inserted into the oyster, which then puts a layer of pearl onto the bead. The thicker the cover, the better the cultured pearl. When tested a solid dark shape showed, with just a light edge, whereas the real pearl let the light through its layers of nacre. In the early days it was quite inexpensive to do, but with the passing years, and the higher salaries, and more elaborate equipment, the cost is now considerable.

The jewellery trade at that time looked upon Freddie as their champion, and when there was any sign of trouble would seek his advice. It was very apparent to me that he was held in high regard in Paris, and I was very proud of him.

We met Paul Marie and his wife for dinner that night in a restaurant on the Champs Elysées. Madame Marie was very soignée, dressed in black and white satin. She had a lovely face, with a very sad expression. Jane liked her very much and we had a very pleasant evening with them.

'Why do French people always entertain one in restaurants Freddie?'

'It is their way. You have to be very close friends to be invited into a French home.'

We left Paris the next day for our tour of the Loire Valley, returning to London at the end of the week. Paris was of course the highlight, and I never forgot my first visit.

I I

European Adventure

Charles McCall decided to continue his travels. Much as he hated to leave Paris, both he and Françoise found it very painful to continue seeing each other, knowing there would be no happy ending. Françoise had a very hard streak, and Charles found her intractable attitude to religion and her willingness to forgo their love, deeply hurtful.

He left for Vienna, which was the perfect antidote. He found the people in the inn where he was staying very friendly; and the gaiety of the city lifted his spirits, and he enjoyed the music and the architecture. It was too vast and impressive for him to find it attractive for his kind of intimate landscape, but the concerts of Mozart, Haydn and Schubert gave him inspiration of another kind.

His next City was Munich. He arrived at the main station, and found a small hotel, which was clean and central. He was struck by the cleanliness of the city,and amused and delighted to see all the dogs had little hygiene baskets strapped to their nether regions. There was no dog pollution on the pavements there! He was wandering along a main street when he suddenly noticed the street empty of pedestrians, and he heard the sound of strident singing, and marching feet. It was a group of Hitler Youth swinging through the town on an exercise. They stopped dead a few yards ahead of him, went into a shop, and came out with a terrified man, being dragged between them. A relative came after them to protest, and was soundly beaten for his trouble. They then painted JUDE on the shop window, and the terrified man was frog-marched away. Charles was horrified and angry and in the pit of his stomach he felt fear. As he watched, people slowly came out of

Peasants Farming in Besigheim, Germany 1937

shop doorways, and went quickly about their business. I do not care for this, he thought, I shall go to the main Art Gallery, and then find a travel agent and leave Munich to the Nazis. As he was going round the Gallery, he ran into two fellow students from Edinburgh. They greeted each other with delight, and went to a local beer cellar for lunch. The beer was strong, and they emerged into the bright sunlight feeling no pain! The town hall of Munich was opposite, and Charles suggested taking their photographs on the impressive steps, the great Nazi flag was at the top. They were delighted with this idea, and ran up the steps, standing in front of the Swastika and clenching their hands in communist salute! They

Near Besigheim German Landscape, Charles McCall 1937

all thought it was a great lark, said their farewells and went on their various ways. Charles went to a travel agent, who advised him to go to a little town on the Franco-German border called Besigheim. 'It is very beautiful there, and it is quiet, and you can sketch and paint the lovely countryside'

He arrived at Besigheim the following evening. His hotel was a small country inn opposite the station. It was a pleasing German rural town. Having installed himself in his room, and washed, he strolled round the streets, getting his bearings, and decided to walk into the fields the next day and start sketching. He looked at his watch, and was irritated to find it had stopped. Across the street he saw a shop with "Wagner, Uhrmacher" on the window. It was a typical German watchmaker's shop, with Wag-at-the-wall cuckoo clocks, and a great clutter of clocks and watches. A small man came into the shop from a back room, 'Do you speak English?' He shook his head, so Charles spoke his halting German, explaining his watch had stopped.

'It needs cleaning, and will be ready by lunch-time tomorrow.'

Charles thanked him and returned to the hotel. His supper was almost raw beef, with sauerkraut and he thought with longing of Madame Dauchez's delicious meals ... The waitress came to remove his plate, and noticed he had not eaten very much.

'Do you not like the food?'

'No, it is too German for me!' he replied in his best German. The girl was highly amused, and returned with a very delicious apple strudel and cream.

'This is good,' said Charles with a grin, and the rosy-cheeked girl went away laughing.

The next day was a crisp September morning, and Charles departed with his portable easel and stool and painting box. He saw a nice composition, went into a field, and settled down to draw and paint. He was immersed in his work, and dimly heard the sound of motor bikes. They stopped on the road, and two men in black uniforms, and polished black boots strode across the field. The stood either side of him, with very menacing faces. 'Ausweis Bitte!' McCall was annoyed, first at the interruption, and secondly at the rude and abrupt request which he did not understand.

'I am British, let me see your papers first!'

Being German they obeyed the command, then said, 'Your passport please.' It was scrutinized. 'Where are you staying?'

He gave the name of the inn.

'This is a fortified area, sketching and photographing are forbidden!'

'I was sent here by a travel agent in Munich to do just this!'

They repeated the warning again, and marched off, climbed on their motor bikes and roared off up the road.

Cursing to himself, he packed up his painting things and returned to the inn. There was just time before lunch to go for his watch.

The watchmaker greeted him with a friendly smile. 'Your watch is ready, sir,' and it was handed to him. As he was fastening it, he told the watchmaker what had occurred. Fear spread over the man's face.

'Sir, you are in grave danger. This is a fortified area. They will never let you go!'

'But I am British, I have a British passport.'

'You may think that will protect you, but believe me, you will meet with an accident, and Hitler will send a wreath. They will not care about you being British!'

At that moment a young boy came into the shop. The watchmaker put a finger on his lips. He served the boy and after he had left, 'One must never speak in front of the young, they are probably Hitler Youth. My Uncle was a waiter in Glasgow, I shall send him to see you at the inn. He speaks very good English and will explain what you must do to escape. I am Jewish and I expect to be bumped off any time!'

Charles returned to the inn deeply concerned. He remembered the incident in Munich, his friends making the communist salute in front of the Swastika. Lord help me! he thought, if they find that I'll be a goner! He ate his lunch in misery and had just finished when the waitress said there was someone to see him. In the hall was a small elderly man with a white beard who spoke with Glasgow accent! 'I have come from the watchmaker. Where can we speak?'

They went to his room. 'I understand from my nephew that you had an encounter with the Gestapo?'

'Yes, I was sketching in the fields by the village, and they said it was a fortified area, and forbidden.'

'You're damn right, you were sketching the Siegfried Line!'

'Christ! I had no idea! The travel agent in Munich sent me here.'

'Well, the first thing to do is get packed. I will help you down with your luggage, and leave it in the hall. Then come to the watchmaker's at three o'clock, and we will plan a safe route for you.'

They took the luggage down, and Charles shook hands with the old man, and went to the desk to pay his bill. As he was standing there, he felt a hand on his shoulder. There stood the local policeman. 'You are the Britisher?' We have had a report about you. Will you come with me to the police station?'

With a sinking heart Charles went with him. The station was a small country police station, and they had just had lunch, and feeling rather sleepy.

Florence 1936

'Why are you here?'

'I am an art student, and I have been travelling through Europe, and was exhausted with the galleries, and just wanted a quiet sketching holiday, and was advised to come here by a travel agent in Munich.' He showed them a pamphlet from the agent.

'Have you taken any photographs?'

'No, as you see I have no camera.' (It was in his luggage at the Hotel).

'I shall report back to my superiors that I think you are a *bona fide* traveller. Leave a forwarding address.'

He left the police station with relief. So far so good.

At three o'clock he went back to the watchmaker. They took him to an upstairs room, and drew the curtains. The watchmaker, his wife, with a baby in arms, (unable to talk!) and the old uncle from Glasgow were all there. They had a large map of the area, and traced out the journey for McCall.

'They will expect you to go the way of your ticket, so you must go in the opposite direction, crossing into France at Wissembourg.'

Once it was all decided Charles thanked them warmly, 'I am very grateful, but I think it will be all right, the police seem satisfied.'

'Believe me, the Gestapo never give up!'

He returned to the inn, paid his bill and went to the station to catch his train. The porter left his luggage on a trolley, and it had to be brought over to the opposite platform. The train was signalled, and there was no sign of him. 'Hell's bells, this is a plot to keep me here.' He felt panic taking hold when suddenly he saw the porter pushing the trolley from the opposite way, just as the train puffed into the station. The luggage loaded on, the whistle blew and he was on his way. Just before he reached the border he heard the inspectors coming up the train. They examined his papers very carefully, and returned them. Shortly after that a French official came in and asked for his papers. 'Are we in France now?'

'But of course, m'sieu.'

To his surprise Charles threw his hat in the air! 'Thank God!' He was so relieved he felt a boil coming on his neck with the anxiety!

Back in his beloved Paris he relaxed under the tender care of Madame Dauchez, who disliked the Germans very much. Strangely Françoise's family rather approved of the Fascist regime, and were members of the French *Croix de Feu*.

The time was coming to return to London and work, but to use his ticket to its greatest advantage, Charles decided to go via Holland, visiting the art galleries there. He was thirsting to see the Rembrandt and Vermeer paintings. He caught the Amsterdam train with all his luggage, and indulged himself with a second-class ticket. A lady was sitting opposite him, and watched with amusement while the porter packed all the bundles of easel and canvases into the carriage, getting most of it up on the wide rack, and the rest under the seat. The whistle blew and the journey began. Charles smiled at the woman opposite, 'I am sorry for all the luggage, but it is the end of a long tour in Europe.'

'I suppose you are English?'

'No Scottish, although I now stay in London.'

'I think you are an artist?'

'Yes, I have been finishing my studies of European art galleries.'

'I am Dutch, and of course am very interested in painting. Where do you think you have found the best art in Europe?'

'That is a difficult question to answer shortly! I was very impressed with Florence, and the little hill towns nearby, like Fiesole, Siena and Arezzo. I was in Spain in 1936, and of course went to Madrid, and was very impressed by the paintings in The Prado.'

'Did you see the Goyas there, and Velasquez?'

'Yes indeed, I have always admired both of these painters. I particularly liked Goya's *Maja Desnuda*, wonderful flesh tones, and Velasquez's famous portraits were thrilling to see. I found Spain a very lonely place, I do not speak Spanish, and was travelling on my own. I also disliked their habit of spitting, which I found disgusting. I left Barcelona the night before the Civil War was declared, and when I arrived at Ventimiglia the Italian security made me strip, because I had come from Spain! I was very angry. Luckily they did not understand English, or I might have been imprisoned.'

'Were you in Paris long?'

'Oh yes, on and off two years. I love France, French painting. It is a strange thing but the Scots have a great affinity with French painting, and paint much more in the French tradition than the English. Something to do with the "Auld Alliance" I suppose!' The woman smiled, and opening her handbag took out a card. 'My husband owned the Kroller-Müller shipping line. Here is my card. Do come and see me one day, and I will show you my collection of van Goghs. They are at present stored in a barn, until we have built a museum for them. They are unknown at the moment, but one day will be well-known.' The train drew in to the station, and she turned to Charles, giving him her elegantly gloved hand. 'Be sure and ring me. I have so enjoyed the journey.'

Charles went to Amsterdam, where he stayed in a small hotel, and visited the major art galleries. It was easy to get around Holland; distances were not great. He telephoned Mrs Müller and arranged to visit her for tea the next afternoon and she arranged to have him met at the station. She lived in an impressive house with great iron gates, and the door was opened by a butler wearing white gloves. Charles was shown into the drawing-room. Mrs

Müller rose to greet him. 'I am so glad you have come. I was afraid you might find too much to do!'

'You intrigued me with the description of your van Goghs in the barn, and it is interesting to see your home.' They had tea, and after she had shown him her personal collection of paintings she opened the French doors, and led him across a yard to a large barn. Inside were rows of canvases, all unframed, stacked like a studio. 'These are the van Goghs!' Charles was horrified at the casual treatment of the paintings, but Mrs Müller was quite happy.

'It is only temporary. Once the museum is built, they will all be framed and hung in the splendour they deserve.' He spent a fascinating hour going through the canvases, finally taking his leave, and thanking his hostess for such an experience.

The next day he left Amsterdam for London.

12

The European travels of Charles McCall, the man I had glimpsed in Pairs and was yet to meet, being over, I shall return to my story.

After the delights of visiting Paris the next important event on my calendar was my 21st Birthday Party in December. Freddie said that I was to have a dance like the others, and preparations began. Marjoie had given birth to a son in September, 1936, who was christened Harry after Charles Marment's father, which did not please Freddie very much. He was delighted with his grandson, and pleased to see he had inherited his blue eyes and fair hair. The little family came and stayed the night of my party.

It was a great success, and I was given so many presents, some wag said it was like a wedding without a bridegroom! I was asked by my Father if I would like a small string of oriental pearls like those my sisters had been given on the same occasion. To his amusement I replied, 'Thank you, Freddie, but I really would prefer diamonds!' So he gave me an exquisite pair of small diamond clips, which I later had redesigned into "fish earrings".

The dance was fun. All our friends came including my cousin Irene, always called "Renee". She was a petite redhead, very like Janet Gaynor the film actress. We always loved her visits, especially when young, as she always led us astray! She was instrumental in finding the cold water tank under our playroom floor, and we played "Pirates" using the tank for "Man overboard". We only put our feet in, as it looked so deep and dark. Jane said, 'I have sent for the plumber, there must be a dead bird in the tank, the water has a funny taste!'

At the age of five I loved to give information. 'Maybe it is because we put our feet in it.' We were all scolded, and forbidden to touch the floorboards again. Renee came to the dance and was a

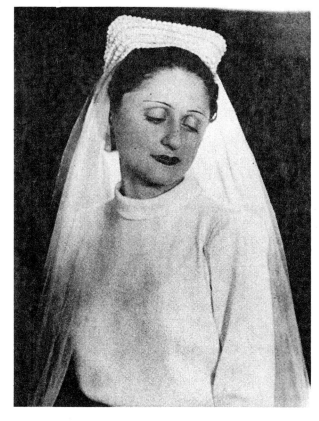

*Yolande Lanvin on her
Wedding day 1938*

great success. Bill, Jo's old flame, was very smitten, but sadly had
to return to Newcastle.

After the excitement life felt rather flat, and I was "difficult",
fighting for my freedom from very strict parental control.

I received an invitation to Yolande's wedding in Paris in the
Spring. After a great tussle, I was allowed to go if I took Maisie,
Freddie's secretary, as chaperone.

We went by boat-train, and it was exciting to be on our own.
We were met in Paris by Paul Marie, who took us to our hotel,
"The Westminster", a modest comfortable hotel behind the
Champs Elysées. The wedding was at St Philippe du Roule, on the
Faubourg St Honoré at noon, the next day. It was a lovely Spring
day, and we dressed carefully for the great occasion.

I wanted to send Yolande flowers on her wedding morning, but
was told by the florist that it was the French custom to send them
to the reception which she knew was to be at the Plaza Athénée at

four o'clock. The church was crowded with very elegant people. Yolande came in looking very serious in her beautiful Lanvin wedding dress. The bridesmaids were very pretty, in blue dresses with flowers in their hair. It was a full Catholic service, and seemed very long. At the end I was surprised to find that the bride and groom waited in the vestry, and we all filed through, giving our congratulations. The close relatives then left with the happy pair for lunch at Jeanne Lanvin's. We all met up again at 4 pm for the reception. The room was a mass of flowers, and Yolande was full of fun. She went round giving pieces of her veil to her close friends, and she gave me a piece. 'For you, Mitzi, for good luck!' I was very pleased.

We were told by Paul Marie that he was to collect us at 8 pm and take us to the Templier home. I was very surprised. 'This is an honour. One is rarely invited to a French home,' I told Maisie, who was very worried because she did not speak French. We were taken as promised, and sat in a real French parlour, on rather uncomfortable chairs. Madame Templier was very formal and spoke no English, which limited things a little. Her pretty daughter, Denise, was very jolly, and could speak English. After sipping an *apéritif*, to my astonishment Paul and Georges Templier rose and announced that they were taking Maisie and myself to dinner! 'Are the ladies not coming?'

'Oh no,' said Paul, 'we do not take our wives to nightclubs!' I could not imagine Jane allowing Freddie to get away with that!

It was a marvellous evening. They took us first to Montmartre and led us round to the steps of the church of Sacre-Coeur to look down on Paris by night. It was magical, just twilight, and all the twinkling lights were shining beneath us. 'Paris has diamonds in her hair!' I said, and they laughed. We went for a little drive, showing Maisie some of the important places. It was her first visit. They then said, we are taking you to dine at "Bal Tabarin". I had heard about it, and asked Freddie to take me, but he had said, 'It is no place for young women!'

We had a table beside the stage, which ran down the centre of the room and there were little steps up onto the stage, so that one could dance after the cabaret. Our hosts ordered the dinner, and we talked excitedly about the things we had just seen, and were having coffee when the lights went out and the stage only was lit. With the scene set for an Eastern Palace the music started with Borodin's "Polovtsian Dances", from *Prince Igor*. To this exciting crescendo of sound Eastern warriors raced in carrying almost nude women, and proceeded to make furious love to them on the tables in front of us! I stole a quick look at Maisie. Her face was a study of frank disbelief that she was witnessing such a scene! As the passion of the music faded the main tableaux of the evening was brought on, supposed to be for the entertainment of the bandits and their captives. The most beautiful girls posed on a half moon, with only glittering stars on their bosoms, and a jewelled G-sting. I took a quick look at the faces round the stage, mostly men's, and I knew then what lust looked like! Several more sensational scenes were enacted, ending with a very lively Can Can!

Paul turned to me and said, 'Well Mitzi, what do you think of our French girls?'

'Absolutely marellous, everything was done with such panache.' The dance music started, a tango which, thanks to lessons from Yolande when I was ten, I could perform with ease. We returned to the hotel about 2 am, happily exhausted. I thought my right knee felt stiff, but was too tired to investigate. We awoke at 9 am and I noticed what looked like an angry red boil starting just under my knee-cap. I showed Maisie. 'I do not like the look of that. What do you think it is?'

'I can only think it is some infection from the fall I had at Waterloo station when I met Freddie from his American trip last week. You remember we washed the wound in the office, and it healed up all right. I never gave it another thought. I shall show it to Dr Rogers when I get home.'

We spent the morning going to Les Invalides and I took Maisie to lunch at the Plaza Athénée. The head waiter was very kind. I explained we were on our own, and that I should like his assistance in choosing lunch. We had melon to start the meal, then cold salmon with salade, and delicious sauce Hollandaise, with new potatoes, followed by *fraises des bois*, all accompanied by a chilled Chablis. It cost me three pounds fifty each, two weeks money, but it was worth it. The head waiter took such pleasure in our enjoyment, and it was a perfect end to our trip.

During the journey my leg began to swell. I was really quite scared, and had a job climbing down the steep steps on the French train. I was glad to get into the train at Dover. Maisie was very worried. 'How will you manage at Victoria?' I was wondering too. It was with great relief and joy I saw Freddie's smiling face on the platform. He and Jane had driven up to meet me!

Dr Rogers came early the next morning. 'I think it is a boil. Get into the hottest bath you can with lots of disinfectant in it and it should burst . . .' That was easier said than done. The bathroom was down a flight of stairs, across a landing, and at the end of a long corridor. I was unable to put my foot to the ground, the pain was awful, so I went on my bottom, with my leg in the air. It amused our maid Mary. I lowered myself into the very hot water, and after a few minutes the beastly thing exploded, like a small volcano! Evil green pus poured out! I nearly fainted. I yelled for Mary, who came racing in, helped me out of the bath. She dried me, and I had the awful journey back to bed. I was so weak and frightened I just burst into tears. We heard the car returning with Jane. Mary raced downstairs. 'Oh Mrs Ward, do come Miss Mitzi is in tears, her leg is something awful!' Jane took one look and rang Dr Rogers. When he saw my leg, he went to the window and whistled under his breath, a bad sign. He turned to me. 'How brave are you? Do you think you could hold onto the bed while I cut it out? The trouble is I have no anaesthetic, and it is an abscess, and must be removed before the poison gets into your blood stream.'

'Please do it, Dr Rogers, it is so sore.'

We sent Jane out of the room, she always fainted at the sight of blood! and I held the sides of the bed, while the Doctor cut out the core of the abscess. He was very quick, and although it hurt, it was such a relief when it was over, I did not mind. 'Good girl, you behaved beautifully. The core was as big as my thumb. It must have been very painful.'

'It was!'

'Well, it is all away now and should heal quite quickly,' Jane came into the bedroom and had a little cry. She could never bear to see any of us suffer. 'Don't cry, Jane, it is all over and I shall be better in no time. Thank God I returned from Paris in time!'

The girls at
Bal Tabarin, 1937

13

In the Spring of 1938, with Hitler marching into Austria, we all had the fear of war at the back of our minds. I thought if it looks like happening, I shall join the WAAF, and keep things in the tradition. It would please Freddie.

In the office we were very busy, and one afternoon Freddie came into my office, his face alive with excitement. 'Just look at these diamonds, you will never see anything finer.' Lying in his hand were two large diamonds, each weighing over fifty carats; the top stone was marquise shape, like the shape of a boat, set in a simple gold setting horizontally. Suspended from the centre was a pear-shaped diamond in the same simple setting. Freddie thought they had come from the Golconda Mines in India because they were so white. 'I am sure they are Indian stones. That Golconda Mine only produced this kind of stone, but often they have carbons, black marks in the stone. I have studied these stones all morning, and even with my strongest loupe have been unable to find a mark!'

'Where have they come from?'

'A bank in the West-End. They want me to make an offer.'

'What do you think they are worth?'

'Almost any money one can think of, but in these difficult times it has to be in relation to holding them over a long period, I should think about twenty-five thousand pounds each!'

'Oh dear, I am afraid they are beyond me! Do you know who is the owner?'

'I am led to believe they belonged to some deposed Eastern Potentate.'

Some days passed and Freddie told me he had bought the stones. 'Which do you think you will sell first?'

'The pear-shape I think.' In fact he sold the marquise almost at

97

once, and it took another year to sell the pear-shape, which we were told went to the same customer.

It often happened that important customers sent for me to go to their house and restring their pearls. I hated it, often one had to cope with snooty servants, who were at a loss to know which drawer to put one in! One agreeable customer had just purchased a pearl necklace for his fiancée, and I was summoned to his flat in St James's. A very acid-faced footman answered the door. 'Miss Ward from Jerwood and Ward, by appointment.'

'The master is not in. What is your business?'

'I have come to restring a pearl necklace. I am expected.'

He sniffed, implying disbelief. 'Come in, you had better sit in the hall!'

He departed to the kitchen quarters, his back stiff with his importance, the gilt buttons shining in his green coat tails. I looked about me, it was all furnished in a very expensive manner, with good antique furniture, and oriental rugs. After about ten minutes I heard a key in the latch, and our young customer came in with his fiancée. She was beautifully dressed, and very pretty. 'Oh Miss Ward, I am so sorry we are late, but we have so many things to buy before the wedding, and time runs away with one. This is my fiancée.'

We were introduced. 'What do you need to work upon?'

'A table and chair, preferably with a baize top. A card table would be excellent.'

'Do come into the drawing-room. Is there anything possible here?'

It was all polished wood surfaces, I could imagine my needle digging in to those! 'Not really, I think I should scratch the surface.' He rang for my enemy.

'Perkins, do we have such a thing as a card table in the flat?'

'Yes sir, in the staff room.'

'Will you please bring it for Miss Ward, and coffee too.'

'Certainly, sir.' The table was duly brought into the room, and the young couple discussed the length the necklace was to be, and left me to complete my task.

I was busy at my desk the next week, when Mr Trehearne, Freddie's partner, came rushing through the door. 'Mitzi, will you jump in a cab and go to Christie's. Take your stringing things. you are to restring a six-row necklace in their rooms. It is a great family heirloom, and they dare not let it out of their sight.' I felt the old panic seize me! I loathed old pearl necklaces, one never knew what problems would rear their ugly heads. Often the pearls are worn, and have large holes where the pearl has worn away, and the rest are tiny. Faced with this situation, the only thing to do is to cut a quill from some game bird's feather, and stick it in. This always guaranteed to get me into "a state".

I duly arrived at 8, King Street. It was a very old building, and Mr Smith, the chief clerk, was at the counter. He was very strict with the young men, and looked very Victorian in his winged collar. 'I have come from Jerwood and Ward to restring some pearls.'

'Oh yes, you are to go with Mr Davidge to the top floor, where we have placed the pearls in a locked room. Mr Davidge will stay with you as bodyguard, and the room is to be locked on all occasions!' I looked at the young man in question, slight in build, with blond hair and a large moustache. His blue eyes were twinkling. 'I am to be your bodyguard,' he said, blushing furiously.

'I shall lead the way. It is up a lot of stairs.'

We eventually came to the top floor, all the corridors were flagstoned, and the room was very dingy. I should not think it was used very much. Mr Davidge locked the door. 'You are safe now.'

'I hope so, I understand the pearls are very valuable.'

'Yes, they are in the box on the table.They were and, as I feared, pretty ancient and with problems. I worked away, and I discovered my bodyguard's name was "Roy," and he was very keen to tell me about the Territorial Army, where he was serving in the Tank Corps. We were just about to stop for lunch, when there was a thunderous knocking on the door. 'Open this door at once!' A loud voice boomed.

'Help, it's Sir Henry!'

Roy Davidge rushed to the door looking very guilty. A large man stood on the threshhold. He looked at me and Davidge. 'What may I ask are you two doing in a locked room?'

I laughed, 'Mr Smith's orders. I am from Jerwood and Ward, and have to string these pearls, and Mr. Davidge is my bodyguard.'

'He glared at me for a second and saw what I said was true.'

'I see. Carry on,' he said and turning on his heel, was gone.

'Whew! You handled that very well. That was Sir Henry Floyd, he was a Colonel in the Hussars, and is very strict.'

'Very military I would say.' We both laughed, and locked the door and went for a sandwich.

At 5 pm we called it a day, and I had been able to complete the work. We went down to the front hall. 'I am sorry the work is finished, I have enjoyed today.'

'I am too, I have not been locked up with the Tank Corps before.'

'I expect I shall see you when I come to your Father's office with goods.'

'I am sure you will. I am always there!' We shook hands, and I left.

I was teased by Maisie and Kinch our commissionaire, and the next time Kinch went to Christies's he made it his business to run into Roy Davidge. He returned with a broad grin, and all sorts of fables about the conversation he had had with Roy. To my astonishment I received a note from him the next morning. It was very flippant, saying he thought the light was red, but a kind gentleman informed him it was green! This started a correspondence which went on until we both left for the war. I would reply by 10 am and Davidge would receive the letter by the 4 pm delivery, and I would have another note upon arrival in the office. It was great fun. Freddie teased me unmercifully. He always ridiculed my boyfriends, in the hope he would put me off! Poor Roy Davidge was terrified of Freddie. He once was caught by Freddie carving into valuable miniatures to see if they were gold, and was thoroughly ticked off. Also he thought we were very rich, and he was afraid to date me.

Maisie and I arranged a tennis party at Shawfield House, with Jack, her friend of the moment, and Roy. It was a lovely day, and I met him at Bickley Station. I made him drive, in case he hated to be driven by a woman. We had a merry afternoon, none of us very good players, and we laughed a lot. In the evening we rolled up the rugs, and danced. Poor Roy was so nervous he trembled like a leaf! I was very amused. Maisie played Chopin on our piano, at which she excelled, and a thoroughly happy evening was had by all. I drove them to the station for the last train, returning in a very happy mood. Freddie and Jane were still sitting in the Drawing room. 'Well did you like him?' Jane said.

'He is not the man for you, much too soft,' Freddie said.

'He will never be able to support you, he has no money, and Christie's is hopeless without a private income!' So I retired to bed, my lovely day spoiled, and very disappointed.

The Summer came and went, and in September we were all very apprehensive of war, and it seemed inevitable. Trenches were being dug, against bombing. We all knew Hitler had a large Air Force.

'Do you think we shall all be wiped out?' I asked at breakfast.

'I think we shall be heavily bombed, but from the fellows in the RAF Club, I gather we have a secret weapon.'

'Really? A kind of death-ray?'

'I have no idea.'

'Freddie, would you drive me to Maidstone, it seems it is the only place I can become a WAAF?'

'You don't want to do that,' Jane chipped in.

'I do, Jane, I am determined to be in a service in wartime.'

'When do you want to go to Maidstone?'

'They say any Thursday.'

'Right we will go on Thursday evening.'

We drove down to Maidstone. Freddie was rather excited to be part of my enlistment. To my disappointment they would not let me join, as I was too far away to drill twice weekly. However, a very nice woman said I could be a "Dormant WAAF" and I should be called up at once should war break out. We returned content that everything was set should disaster strike.

The next week Chamberlain flew to Munich, and returned with his fluttering piece of white paper which was supposed to be Peace. 'It will give us time to arm,' said Freddie despondently. Everywhere one heard "Umbrella Man". I wondered what would happen to the theatres. I still remembered seeing the wonderful production of Romeo and Juliet in 1935 with John Gielgud as Romeo, and Peggy Ashcroft as Juliet. Laurence Olivier was Mercutio and Edith Evans the Nurse. It was an experience I shall never forget. I had no idea English could be so beautiful, or Shakespeare so entrancing. I went to everything I could afford, my taste was very catholic. I enjoyed Noël Coward's plays and Ivor Novello's musical extravaganzas wonderfully staged at Drury Lane, any good play, and Promenade concerts. I wanted to see everything I could.

Roy and I went to the cinema together. It was a truly platonic friendship. I suspected he was growing fond of me, but I felt no urge to speed things on their way. Our mutual strong sense of humour stopped any sloppiness. In August, 1939 he rang me at the office, he caught me in the front office under Freddie's eagle eye, and ears! 'I have drawn all my money out of the bank. I think war is near and I shall take you out every night until it is spent!'

'Oh Roy, I can pay my share.'

'Nonsense, I have been alerted for call-up and this is what I want to do. Can you meet me tomorrow, and what would you like

The Five Row Pearl necklace bought by Freddie just before the 1930 crash for £57,000

to see?'

'Yes I can, I should like to go to "The Empire" and see *Goodbye, Mr Chips*.'

'OK, meet you at 5.30 pm.' I put down the telephone. Now parting was so near, I did not want him to leave. Freddie, studying my face, said, 'What was all that about?'

'Roy has been alerted for call-up and he wants to take me out every night until he is posted.'

Freddie wrinkled his nose. 'No need to rush things. Keep your head clear. It is no time to get married.'

'I have not been asked. I do not think he has that in mind.'

We went out together, and I knew he was slightly in love with me. The film was very sad, and he laughed because I had shed a tear. 'Let's go to "The Corner House" and have a bite.' All too soon it was time to catch my train from Victoria. We stood holding hands, and with a quick hug he was gone.

Freddie asked me to go into the front office and restring the

Freddie in the Office

"Five Row". It was a massive five-row pearl necklace with a huge sapphire and diamond cluster snap. It had come from the Russian crown jewels. Freddie had bought it just before the 1930 crash for £57,000. 'If it is likely you may be called up, I thought you had better restring the necklace before you go!'

I had just finished it when the 'phone rang. Freddie answered. 'It's for you.'

'Hallo?'

'It's me, I have been called-up. I leave for Salisbury plain tonight! So regretfully I can't meet you.'

'Oh Roy, do take care, I expect I shall get called-up now.'

'Keep in touch. I shall send you my address.'

I put down the 'phone. Freddie was watching me. 'He's called up, so our little rendezvous did not last very long.'

Freddie said, 'It looks as if war is very near.' I thought sadly, this is the end of a chapter, what will happen to us all now?

14

McCall becomes a Soldier

Charles McCall and I were still not known to each other, although our paths were drawing closer and our inevitable meeting coming nearer.

Charles McCall settled down in his Redcliffe Road Studio. He worked passionately, from first light until it faded. He was happy, never gregarious and enjoyed the long days struggling to put the pictures in his mind onto canvas. Nora Smith invited him in to her studio to share her models, and three important paintings were the result. The first model was an American student they called Mac, a large blond man, studying literature and philosophy and always surrounded in the evening by adoring females. He was a good model, with large shapes and strong features. Remembering Peploe's "Get the planes right", Charles painted quickly, and finished the painting measuring 30x25 in two hours. Nora said, 'That is very good Charles. Don't touch it, it is a complete statement.' Mac did not like it, and preferred a more formal portrait, which was painted later, and bought it. There was a young man who was looking for work, so Nora, who was always very kind, while pretending to be tough, asked him to model. He had not the attraction of Mac, but was very paintable. Charles painted a strong picture of him, and put it into the Royal Academy Summer Exhibition of 1939, where it was hung and received favourable reviews. Charles was encouraged, and shared a professional model with Nora called Maxine. He painted two paintings of her, a three quarter length nude, which was made for him because it was very cold in the Studio, and he gave her a striped dressing gown to tie round her hips. Immediately he saw a picture. Maxine was Malayan, and it looked like a sarong! It was again painted quickly, and was to be one of his paintings he

Old Jim, this picture was destroyed by fire in Suffolk, 1943

prized. He also painted a small head at the same time. Then war was declared. They all discussed what was the best plan. Charles decided he would stay in London until the bombing started, and at the invitation of his friend, the writer Harold Freeman, sent many paintings to Suffolk to be stored in a barn for safety. The barn burned down during the War, and all the paintings were destroyed. All that remains of the burnt pictures is an old photograph of "Old Jim".

Charles lead the usual Chelsea life in the evenings, and Nora said she was going to give a fancy dress party in her studio. Charles and his current girl friend went as Adam and Eve. The drinking was liberal, and passions became inflamed. To McCall's anger he saw another artist making love to his "Eve"! He was so cross he grabbed the fellow by the scruff of the neck. The culprit was unable to hold onto him as Charles was nude, except for a small pair of pants with a fig leaf, fore and aft! So he easily disposed himself of his adversary by throwing him down the stairs . . .

At one of the Christmas parties, a friend of Charles called Eddie Gray invited him to supper at his club. During dinner he invited him to put up for Camouflage in the Royal Engineers. 'You will be commissioned, and then they will send you wherever they need a spot of camouflage. You are bound to be called up soon. Why not get into something you have a clue about?' It made sense, so he signed the form, and awaited results. Early in 1940 he received instructions to report at Shorncliffe Barracks in Folkestone, to train to be a soldier!

Having kitted himself out at Harrods, McCall arrived at the Barracks looking every inch a soldier! but that was as far as it went. He met a delightful man called Patrick Phillips, a good painter of portraits and landscape. Patrick had been to OTC at Eton, and took the green McCall under his wing. Charles had to shave off his black beard, and now wore a trim military moustache. Patrick was very amused at McCall on the drill square. After the course he was immediately posted to Edinburgh. He was very pleased, and was able to sneak off to Nigel McIsaac's studio in Church Lane, and do some painting when off duty. The CO was a rabid Scot, and refused to have a Campbell in his mess, as he was a MacDonald! The massacre in Glencoe of 1692 was still in his mind.

Charles was placed in a team with a Captain, and they toured the Highlands together, camouflaging military and naval outposts. It was the first time he had met someone he really detested. The

Captain was a rogue. To Charles' dismay he found he had stolen his favourite penknife. It alerted him to the man's character. He also found that the gallant Captain was leading a very pretty little Wren (Women's Royal Navy) up "the garden path". Charles knew he was married, and was dismayed when the poor girl told him she was pregnant, and the Captain was to marry her the next week! She even bought the wedding-dress, and then the army caught up with the villain, and he was cashiered. Charles was called as a witness, and found the whole thing repellent. He thought he saw his first white hair after this episode!

Charles was posted to London and the bombing had started in earnest. Luckily, he always seemed to be out of London on the really bad raids, but would be horrified by all the destruction upon his return. His HQ was in Queens Gate. He was very fond of the middle-aged ladies there, who were very kind to him. He was sent next to Matlock, with the promotion of Captain. His Major was a merry man called Walton, a Northerner who made enemies through being overbearing. However, as a companion in the Mess, Charles found him amusing. Walton was highly amused when Charles, having a bad attack of fibrositis, presented himself before the MO and could not recall the name of his complaint. 'I have the frenzies!' he said. After several months he was posted to Belfast.

The crossing to Northern Ireland was uneventful, for which he was truly grateful, as he was Officer in Charge, being the senior rank on board. The food was wonderful after England, and apart from lecturing the troops on camouflage, which they found very boring, until he cunningly put a few nude drawings between the slides, all he had to do was inspect the gunsites. He met a painter in Belfast called Sidney Smith. A quiet fellow, who was very kind and allowed him the use of his studio when he was able to be free. After a few months he was posted to Kimberley, near Nottingham. That was a nice interlude, he thought. I wonder what delights Kimberley has to offer?

15

The Second World War

We were all expecting an announcement from the Prime Minister on Sunday, 3rd September. The smell of roast beef floated through from the kitchen and it all seemed so normal. Neville Chamberlain told us we were at War. We were stunned, somehow one never thought it would really happen. Cherry and I had spent the morning packing all the Venetian glass into trunks, carefully wrapped in newspaper. Much to Freddie's irritation we had used that day's *Sunday Times*! Jane said, I think you should go and get Eva and Eve. If the bombing starts, they should be with us in the cellar. Off I went in the car to Bromley to collect them. Auntie Eva was very reluctant to come. However, I said that lunch would spoil, so why not come and discuss it with Jane as she was so worried? We were just closing the door, when the air-raid siren wailed its warning! 'Quick jump in the car!' I drove like one possessd. The roads were empty, one had been told to stop and immobilize one's car in an air raid! Along Plaistow Lane an air-raid warden in full gas clothing tried to stop me. I drove straight at him and he leapt up the wall. The last I saw was him hanging on the fence!

We arrived at Shawfield House just as the all clear sounded. They were all standing at the door. Jane was in tears with fright and worry. Everyone calmed down and we went in to lunch.

The Air Ministry letter arrived on Saturday, 9th September asking me to report to RAF Hendon on the following Monday, 11th September, to be enrolled. It caused a little consternation. Jane cried, and Freddie said, 'Come with me this morning we will go to the Club for lunch.'

I tidied my desk in the office, leaving Maisie a few stringing tips, and making sure all the needles were threaded. The little French girl who sat in the window opposite mine, across the street, polishing jewellery all day, waved frantically when in sign language I told her I was off to the War. She had been so delighted last Christmas when I had sent her one of the many boxes of chocolates I had received, and I was touched when she in return sent a bunch of violets.

We left for the RAF Club and it felt like the last day at school. I knew Freddie was rather miserable about the coming break, and tried to cheer him up. We were both wearing our civilian gas masks, gruesome things, which made us all look like pigs, and wrecked one's hair style! They were in cardboard boxes on a string, and certainly did nothing for one's appearance. All through the West End the sandbags were being placed around places of importance, sticky paper in criss-crosses was over the glass windows, and blackout curtains covered hotel windows. It was all very depressing. In the Club suddenly nearly everyone was in uniform. I thought how quickly things change. Will our London really be flattened, as Hitler promises?

'Freddie, have you heard from Allie?'

'Yes, he was on the 'phone this morning. He wants you and Cherry to go to America for the duration.'

'It is very kind of him, but it is unthinkable that I would go and leave you and our country at such a time.'

'That's what I thought, but I said I would put it to you and ring him tonight.'

'He really is a true friend, but no one can appreciate this kind of situation without experiencing it. Logically it is a good idea, but logic and feelings don't mix!'

Freddie nodded gloomily. 'Let's change the subject. Tell me about your most amusing experience in New York,' I said. He took a long sip from his dry Martini.

'Well, I suppose the night after Muff Munro's wedding. I had arranged to meet Allie at Texas Guinnan's club after the wedding, and in white tie and tails and a white carnation in my button-hole, I took a cab to the club. I must admit I was feeling very merry. Much champagne had been consumed. I arrived at the revolving door, and went round twice because it was rather fast! The second time round I was on the carpet in a run. There was no sign of Allie and Texas Guinnan was on stage. She stopped the show, addressing me. "Can I help you, fella."

"I am looking for Allie." "Give the boy a hand. He's lost his bride!" Everybody laughed and clapped. I walked up to the stage,

all the way exchanging repartee. I arrived at the stage,
'What's your name fella,'
'Freddie.'
'Gosh, Freddie, you really are a dude!' She came down to meet
me, I kissed her hand. "Listen everybody, this is a real English
gentleman. He will sit at my table, and we shall give him an
evening to remember!'
'How fantastic. What happened?'
'She was wonderful, gave me dinner with champagne, and we
had a very good party. When it was time to go, I stood up to say
my farewells. She refused to take any money, and sent me back to
"The Plaza" in her black Rolls Royce!'
"I certainly would love to go to New York after the war.'
'You will, you see.'
Freddie looked very thoughtful. 'You know, to get back to this
situation we are all facing, it will be tough, but the only way to
take it, is to look on it as a Greek tragedy. When bad things
happen, as they must, try not to take it too much to heart. Think it
will pass and try and concentrate on the things of the moment.'
'It is going to be such a different life, I expect my old school
discipline will help,' I said.
'Yes, try and keep out of trouble, especially with NCOs!'
Lunch being over, we left for home. On Sunday evening we had
had supper, and the garden was looking beautiful. Freddie asked
me to go into the garden with him. I knew he wanted to speak
about sex and morals, but he had always been loath to speak about
these things to his daughters. We walked slowly over the lawn.
'Darling, I just want to warn you of some of the dangers the future
holds for you. You will be with a lot of men, from all walks of life.
They will flatter you, pretend they love you, all for one thing, and
when they get it you will not see them again! So be wise, and
careful, and never do anything you would be ashamed to tell me
about.'
'Don't worry, Freddie, I am quite intelligent, and have no
illusions about myself. It will have to be a real love match before I
succumb.'
He sighed with relief. 'Well that's got that off my chest, let's go
and have a liqueur to toast your future.'
The next morning I took a tearful farewell from Jane, and
travelled with Freddie to London. He said that he wanted to put
me on the underground to Colindale. We arrived at Charing Cross,
Freddie carried my large pigskin suitcase, and I carried the small

pigskin Gladstone bag, both twenty-first presents. We arrived on the platform and I gave Freddie a great hug, and entered the train. Tears were streaming down his face. It really upset me, he had never cried for me before. The train sped away. I sat on the seat trying not to cry. One tear trickled down my cheek, but I managed to keep back the rest. The woman opposite was staring at me. I turned away and looked at the reflections, and gradually got myself under control.

At Colindale I asked the way. 'You can't miss it, love. Up that long road and the guardroom is at the end.' As I struggled up the road with my heavy case I thought, no more Jane to drive me everywhere, this is life in earnest! I reported at the guardroom. A nice woman in RAF sergeant's uniform was sitting at a table. I gave her my letter, 'Oh yes, Ward, we are expecting you, please go to married quarters No. 24, which you will share with two other women, and report back here at 11 am sharp. I went back up the road to No 24. The door was open and I walked in. An attractive blonde girl was sitting on a bed, and a thin dark girl standing by the window.

'I am Mitzi Ward, I have been told to come here.'

The blonde rose smiling. 'That's right, your name is on our list. That is your bed against the wall, and the green tin thing is your locker for your clothes. I am Vicki and this is Rosalie. I am a crooner, and she is an artist's model. What do you do?'

'I am a pearl stringer.'

'What on earth is that?'

'I string pearls in the jewellery business.'

They laughed. I unpacked and slid my case under the bed. The bed was iron, with three squares called "biscuits", a ghastly hard sheet, and brown blankets. The others had made up their beds, mine was all stacked up. 'Let me help you make up the bed.' Vicki came over, and in no time it looked more comfortable. They then asked me where I lived, and told me about themselves. They both lived in London. Vicki was a professional singer, she looked the part with very blonde curls, and very made up with jammy lipstick on her generous mouth. Rosalie was attractive, slim about 5' 7" in height, much more reserved than Vicki. She had an interesting face, with eyes that seemed to run up at the corners. I liked them both. We all went along at 11 am and were told to form four lines. We looked an odd lot, all in our civilian clothes. The same WAAF Sergeant was in charge. "Attention!" Some did; mostly they did not obey the command. so it was carefully explained and we tried again. We were told to be ready at 2 pm for medicals. At 4 pm for issue of what uniform was available. Supper at 7 pm. Lights out at 9 pm. Reveille at 6 am. Parade at 7 am.

Back in our house Vicki said, 'Some odd balls there, did you see that great Lesbian?'

'What's that?'

'A woman who sleeps with women!'

'I've never heard of that.' Rosalie laughed.

'Where have you been all your life?'

'Rather sheltered I am afraid.'

Vicki said, 'Have you got a lover?'

I was rather shaken, 'No, a boy friend.'

'You mean you don't sleep together?'

'Certainly not! We are very platonic!'

'Oh Lord, we are going to have to look after you.' They both laughed. We went to bed. There was a primitive basin in a back room and a loo. We had to go to the ablutions for a bath, I was told. After the orderly officer had been round to check we were all in, I was just settling down for the night on the very hard bed, when to my astonishment Rosalie disappeared out of the window. She returned at 5 am. Vicki said she had gone to be with her lover. I thought this life is certainly going to be different.

The medical was a little shattering, the MO was in RAF uniform, extremely good-looking, and it seemed very odd to expose one's all to this good-looking stranger. The rest was academic. Drilling, in dreadful WAAF issue shoes, and my poor feet were so sore. Vicki suggested we should go and buy our own, which we all thought a brilliant idea. I bought a nice pair of soft leather with crepe soles, and life was a lot easier after that. We were drilled by an RAF flight sergeant. He was very sarcastic and strict, and when a rat ran across the tarmac where we were drilling, and we broke ranks screaming, he ranted and raved about discipline!

I received a letter of congratulations from Dr Hardman our Rector at Chislehurst, wishing me well in the forces. I thought Vicki and Rosie, as we now called her, would never stop laughing. We had our selection interview for "Trade".

'What do you fancy doing, Ward?'

'Driving?'

'Have you driven for three years, and can you change a wheel?'

'No, ma'am.'

'That's out!'

'Would you like to be a plotter?'

'What's that, ma'am?'

'Oh, I think you go with the squadrons to France, and plot their courses for them.'

'Yes, I think I should like that.'

'Right, you will go to Leighton Buzzard to learn your trade. I should like you to scrub out this office this afternoon.'

'Yes, ma'am.'

I returned in the afternoon and was given a scrubbing brush, kneeling pad and a bucket of water. I had never scrubbed a floor before. Of course, in no time I had a flood of black mud! I struggled with it for an hour and at last it was clean and dry. I was very proud of it. 'Look Sergeant, isn't it clean?' 'Marvellous job, Ward, do the Officer's room tomorrow!' Lesson No. 1 — never do a good job of unpleasant tasks!

We left for Leighton Buzzard by transport, all packed into a large truck. It seemed to be hundreds of miles away, and we were finally put down in the drive of a large house. We were four to a room, and I must say they were nicer than the married quarters. We went down to tea, and to our astonishment were only given one piece of bread. We were all starving. Supper was worse. Girls were fighting for the scraps of meat in the "stew". I wrote home, and said we were starving. It was true. We went on 7 mile route-marches to return to one piece of bread. Then my luck shone for me. Who should be in the kitchen but the little French girl from the office opposite in Hatton Garden! We greeted each other with open arms. I told her we were starving, and she smuggled sandwiches up to my room each night. A great parcel of cakes and biscuits arrived from Jane.

It had all been eaten in half an hour, we were so hungry! I had also written a very funny letter to the Sergeant in Hendon about our plight. She showed it to the WAAF Officer there who immediately reported it to Air Ministry. They investigated and found the WAAF Officer in charge at Leighton Buzzard was spending the ration money on furnishing the hostel! Suddenly we were fed properly, and the ordeal was ended. Our course concluded, we were all posted all over the country. I was sent to Fighter Command at Stanmore.

16

Stanmore

We all arrived by RAF transport at Stanmore. We were met by the WAAF Officer. 'I do apologise to you all, but we have been unable to find you the accommodation we require, so as a temporary measure we are putting you all in these workmen's cottages. The snag is they only have double beds!'

The girl standing next to me turned quickly, 'Share with me for God's sake!' Slightly surprised, I agreed. The reason became very obvious when the only two who had not paired off were two Lesbians of the same persuasion.

My bedfellow was an attractive girl called Pat Woollam. She had very red hair, and came from Gloucestershire. We both laughed about the double bed, and put a bolster down the middle to stop kicking each other. We soon found we were on different four hour watches which rotated through the night, so it was not often we were both off duty together.

We were all kitted out with uniform. They were so ghastly that Pat and I went to London and had ours made. The underwear was unspeakable, cheap bright pink sateen bras and navy bloomers. We fell about laughing. I put mine in a drawer in their packets, and returned them in the same condition when I was commissioned two years later.

I was in Operations room 1. Vicki was in Operations room 2, and although we met in the ablutions, very rarely saw each other. Our Ops room was run by a Flight Sergeant Vialls, a tall gipsy-looking man, with a very hot temper. We were allowed only five minutes break per four hour watch, and Vialls would time us with a stop-watch! We had to run up a flight of stairs, try and get in the loo, there were always several from Ops 2 up there, and back downstairs before he clicked his watch. He would give a satanic laugh to see us scurrying up and down the stairs.

At first there was very little to do on duty, no enemy raids. We were told to knit. I am no good at knitting and started a scarf for Roy in his Tank Corps colours, which sadly I never finished.

There was a large RAF corporal with small piggy eyes in charge of our watch. To my horror he made advances to me. It was a real dilemma. If I was nasty he could give me all kinds of horrid tasks. As I feared, I was invited out to the pictures in Watford. I exaggerated my relationship with Roy as a protection, but it did not save me from a most undignified tussle at the garden gate upon our return, and I was told I was a stuck-up bitch, which I thought was a little unfair. When I next went on duty, he put me on to scrubbing the Ops room floor, which was about 120 feet square. Armed with my scrubbing brush and bucket, I started. The controller was a middle-aged Wing Commander who hated noise, so I made a frightful clatter on each wooden stair up to the balcony. 'Take that woman off the fatigue. She is making too much noise!' I looked at the Corporal with an innocently bland face. He was very angry.

I was astonished to have a visit from my godfather, Edward Jerwood, complete in red tabs of a staff officer. He was ADC to General Willens. 'Come and have lunch, I have a staff car, and tell me how you are making out.' We had a pleasant meal, and he took me on to an ENSA concert. We could not sit together because I was in the ranks, and he embarrassed me by turning round at every interval and waving!

We were moved before Chistmas to a small house opposite the "Huts" where the main camp was in Elstree Lane. We were all "A" Watch, which made it easier for sleeping, and four of us shared a room. It was a very cold winter, and there was no heat in the house. The hot water only did two baths, and there were thirty of us in the house. We had a visit from HRH the Duchess of Gloucester. By that time I was a Corporal and she asked me what conditions were like. To the WAAF officer's horror I told her. She was charming, and agreed it would not do, and rotas must be arranged, and the boiler kept on all day. To my sruprise it all happened, and life was much easier. As a Corporal I was in a two room, with a very nice girl, only eighteen, called "Willi", as her name was Williams. She was also a Corporal. She was very delicate, and suffered bronchial asthma in the cold. I looked after her with Jane's pet potions, and we were good friends. Then the bombing started in earnest. I would have to stand by the duty bus at 9 pm with the shrapnel from the guns running off the roof, in order to make the rest wear their tin hats! They hated squashing their curls.

Roy and I had continued to meet until he was posted overseas. Sadly there had been a disagreement before he left, and I did not quite know the score. I discovered much later, through Maisie, that Freddie had warned him off.

As the bombing increased, we had less and less sleep. One of the girls on my watch was only fifteen, she had lied about her age, and was quite hysterical with fright. So I would get up and go into the rooms, trying to give comfort. One night a land-mine on a parachute exploded in the field next door, leaving a crater big enough for a London bus. I was standing at the top of the stairs. All the lights were on and the blackout closed, when there was an almighty bang, and I found myself standing downstairs in the hall! All the windows were blown in, the curtains in shreds. I dashed into the lower room, and all I could see were four bottoms sticking out from under the beds. They all emerged unhurt. I dashed up to the next floor. My little friend was having hysterics. I comforted her, and the next day requested she should be posted to a "quiet" place. This was done. It was a strange fact that Miss Davies' quotation "Keep the centre calm" so often turned blank terror to laughter, and saved the day. On duty it was frantic. I was "lines", working the switchboard, and the switch of telephone lines through Leighton Buzzard, should communication be broken through bombing. An Irish RAF Sergeant was my boss. 'Jesus Christ, the only woman who can connect the Admiralty with Douglas Wood,' a small station in Scotland, and all said in a broad Irish accent! It was not true. I managed very well, and every night Air Chief Marshall Dowding would come to me and say, 'What is the state of the lines, Corporal?' He was a marvellous man, and knew everyone's job in the Command. It was very obvious to us that we had a tough fight on our hands. The Fighter pilots took on enormous odds, and after Dunkirk, and Churchill's great speech, which I listened to in a small pub in Bushey, we all thought it was just a matter of time before German boots were heard in Whitehall.

I was off duty on 28th June, 1940, when a fighter pilot friend of mine walked into the hostel garden. He had come to pick up Stella, his fiancée, 'Mitzi, what on earth is your father up to? I heard he had bought a diamond necklace today for £24,400, sold for the War Effort at Christie's. Evidently the only time they have had a sale for one article!' I was astonished. 'First I have heard of

The diamond necklace, sold by Christie's for the war effort on 28th June 1940

it. I shall ring home tonight and find out what it is all about.'

I telephoned Freddie. 'What have you been doing?'

'I bought a large diamond necklace given by an American lady for the War Effort. It was nearly a fiasco. She had offered a pearl necklace of the same value, and I knew we should never get that figure at the moment for pearls, and I asked Christie's if they could ask her to switch it for diamonds, which luckily she was able to do!'

'Yes, and Christie's were in a funk at the last minute. They had word the "ring" was going to operate, and they feared they would not get the money. I told them not to worry, I was determined to buy it!'

'Marvellous, Freddie. Wasn't it strange a fighter pilot picked it up on his radio returning from a raid, and knew me?'

'Funny old world. When are you coming home?'

'I hope in about two weeks I shall get a break.' We rang off.

It was a frantic Summer, marvellous weather. On the 7th September we came off duty at midnight, and from Stanmore Hill it looked as though the whole of London was on fire. It was very

A MAGNIFICENT DIAMOND NECKLACE

PRESENTED BY A LADY

to the Nation as a Contribution towards the
Cost of the War Effort

(Sold by Order of the Lords Commissioners of the Treasury)

WHICH

Will be Sold at Auction by

MESSRS. CHRISTIE, MANSON & WOODS, Ltd

(Gordon Hannen, Sir Henry Floyd, Bart., Sir Alec Martin, I. O. Chance,
The Rt. Hon. John Gretton, M.P. and R. W. Lloyd.)

AT THEIR GREAT ROOMS

8 KING STREET, ST. JAMES'S SQUARE,
LONDON, S.W.1

On FRIDAY, JUNE 28, 1940

at TWELVE NOON precisely

May be viewed Four Days preceding, and Catalogues had, at
Messrs. CHRISTIE, MANSON AND WOODS' Offices, 8 *King Street*,
*St. James's Square, London, S.W.*1

TELEPHONE: WHITEHALL 8177 (PRIVATE EXCHANGE)
TELEGRAMS: CHRISTIART, PICCY, LONDON

ILLUSTRATED CATALOGUE

Christie's Catalogue

horrifying. The next week was very hard going. We never stopped
at work. On September 15th I was on the telephone to my WAAF
friends at Ventnor. They were giving me information. 'Have you
any enemy bombers near you?'

'Corporal is going outside to look. He says there are three
Spitfires heading towards us very low. Scrap that, they are ME
109s. Excuse the noise. We are going under the table.' There was a
great clatter as their headsets tangled with their tin hats, then
silence. They had been wiped out. I felt very sick. When I came off
duty they said, 'Come to the dance,' so I went. I did not want to
think. At the dance the Wing Commander took the microphone. 'I
am sure you will all rejoice that today the RAF shot down 1,733
German bombers. Our losses were 915.' We all cheered, but the
sorrow stayed in my heart.

We were all looking so neat in our bought uniforms that it
angered the WAAF CO and when the next pay parade came
round, it was always on Saturday morning, it was posted in DRO
(Daily Routine Orders) that all WAAF personnel would appear in
issue uniform! There was consternation at first. Then we got a
bright idea. We would do exactly as was ordered, and it was
hilarious, our skirts down to our ankles, no make-up, hats pulled
down over our ears. It looked like 1914! We all did it, so everyone
looked a sight, and we marched on parade. It was taken by the
RAF Station Commander, and the WAAF Officer commanding.
We all had to go up to the table, say our name and number, and
salute. We all did it with dead-pan faces. At the end of the parade
the RAF CO turned to the WAAF officer and said, 'What has
happened to the usual smart band-box WAAF I see?'

'They are wearing their issue uniforms on my orders!'

'Right, tell them to wear their own uniforms, I never want to see
my WAAFs looking like that again!' With a sigh of relief we all
packed the dreaded garments back into our kit bags.

Lofty Vialls of stop-watch fame was commissioned and sent to
the East Coast training station as a Squadron Leader. Before he
left, he called me into his office. 'I am going to ask for four NCOs
to help me in training, and I thought it would give those of you
who have had a tough time a respite from the bombing, and I am
going to put in for you as one. Are you interested?'

'I should love it. When shall we be sent for?'

'During October. It will be for three weeks.'

True to his word, I received instructions to report at RAF
Bawdsey the first Monday in October. Four of us were going: Anne

Harland, Hilda Shooter, Paddy Moore and me. It was in rather holiday mood that we set off. We found we were the only service women on the coast, as they expected an invasion any time. There was a ferry across the river to the camp, and the ferry-man had orders that should the invasion occur he was to take us at speed up river. We had to sleep with our gas clothing with tin hats beside our beds.

During the day we taught the middle-aged RAF to plot. In the evening we would all meet in "The Ferry Boat Inn", which was very old Suffolk, with small beamed rooms, and great fires. One of the "pupils" was an artist called Iain MacNab who had served in the First World War in the Argyle and Sutherlands and been very badly wounded. He loved to tell us about his wife, Helen, who was a dancer, 'Much younger than me' and I was very amused by this, and imagined a *'Folies-Bergère'* type. When I finally met Helen, she was very serene and stately, and taught ballet and ethnic dances.

Mac loved to teach us all to drink 'Rum Catalan' which involved rum and sugar, and setting light to it. Two other pupils came along, a Mr Meyer who was a bridge expert, and "Jumbo" Napier, who seemed to be "something in the City". At the end of their course they invited us and "Lofty" to a splendid dinner dance at "The Felix Hotel". It was a delightful evening, but the next morning when we met Lofty, he was in a rage. 'Don't you all understand, that was a giant bribe for soft postings.' Personally, I thought it was a lot of fuss about nothing. Anyway, poor MacNab and Meyer were posted to Kirkwall, and Napier to Fighter Command.

We had another strange incident. We were all summoned to Lofty's office and he was obviously in a black rage, and kept us standing in silence whilst he viciously kicked a tobacco tin round the floor. He then looked up. 'It has come to my ears that a WAAF was seen walking about the camp last night! I find this an affront to my trust. I did not expect you girls to let me down. Now look me in the eyes and answer the truth. Was it you Anne?'

'No, sir.'

He looked at me quite obviously sure it was me! 'Was it you, Mitzi?'

'No sir!'

Slight relief passed over his face. 'Was it you, Shoot?'

Poor "Shoot" was trembling, 'Yes Lofty, but I can explain.'

'Well?'

'I wanted to go to the operations room and see the crew at work

The Woodcut, Ferry Boat Inn, Bawdsey, Suffolk by Iain McNab

at night. There was nothing sinister about it.'

'You have the nerve to tell me there was nothing wrong in one of my trusted WAAF NCOs walking about an entirely male camp at night? Where is your sense, woman?'

'I am sorry, sir, I just never thought.'

'Well, I am glad it is no worse, but anymore breaking of curfew and back you all go to the bombing!'

I turned to Anne. 'Gosh, I am glad it wasn't me. He had my punishment all ready I am sure. He was quite put off when it was "Shoot".

Anne laughed. 'Well, he thought you were the most likely to be naughty!'

'Anne, that's not fair,' but I knew what she meant.

In the Spring the first batch of us were sent to Bawdsey for training as Officers in our work, and it was very intensive, with great scientists like Julian Huxley lecturing us. When we had passed our examination at the end of the course, we were warned not to get married, as it had cost so much to train us! It had been a very lively time. That part of the coast was defended by the

Highland Light Infantry. They were a wild lot, and we tried never to go out with any officer unless several of us were together. Willi had come as "Staff" and to get her rest from bombing a whole crowd of my friends were on the course, so it was great fun in the evenings. We were all taught the eightsome reel, and very hot it was dancing in uniform in a blacked out Nissan hut. We were all invited to the HQ of the regiment on Easter Sunday. It was at Woodbridge, and an army truck was sent for us. It was a large house, with the lawn running down to the river. The pipe band marched up and down, and we all had drinks on the lawn. My friend Elizabeth Stone had become very attached to one of the quieter officers called David Taylor, but at that party David got very merry, and pulled my corporal's stripes off my uniform, much to my irritation, they are tricky to sew on, so I threw his subaltern's pips into the bushes! He had a terrible search to find them. We all thought it a very good party.

Willi and Paddy Moore and I were wandering through the grounds, Paddy and I had our white cadet's bands on our caps. Willi was still a corporal, she went on the next course. We heard the air raid warning, but it was always for ships being bombed offshore, so paid no heed. Suddenly there was the sound of diving aircraft. I shouted, "Run" and we all three jumped as one into a small dugout. The bullets thumped into the earth above us! We were all roaring with laughter at our instant reaction, then had a slight shiver at our narrow escape! Willi said, 'They must have seen your white hat bands!'

We returned to London the next day.

We had our Officer Board in Whitehall, and were asked the usual questions of school and background. They said, 'We notice you are a Corporal. What do your duties concern?'

'I have fifty-six airwomen on my watch, and am responsible for their health and general safety, their ability to perform their duties, and to supply my officers with all the back-up they require.'

'Is there no sergeant?'

'No, ma'am, all the NCOs in charge of the four Watches are corporals.'

While I was on my Officers' training course, my old rank was made up to Sergeant.

We all passed the course, and the "Queen WAAF" came for our passing out parade. I was taken to lunch by Denise Robins, whose daughter Pat was on the same course. She told me she lived at 1, Caroline Terrace, SW1, near Sloane Square in London. I had no idea where it was, but stangely I lived in the house next door twenty years later!

I was posted to Nottingham.

17

Watnall Near Nottingham

I arrived in Nottingham after two days in Preston, to which they found I had been sent in error. I was relieved. At first I was put in the WAAF Officers' Mess, in a spare room while the officer was away.

*Mitzi. Commissioned in 1941
Photographed at Watnall*

I found the atmosphere friendly, but very "jolly hockey sticks". The CO had been a school mistress, and her second in command also. They were quite a lot older than me and I was frankly bored. On duty, which was in an old Chapel, our RAF Officer in command was Tony Hankey who had been a film producer in private life, a charming man, with a great sense of humour, and wit. He had just married a WAAF called Mollie. I was somewhat a creature of interest, being the first WAAF Officer to arrive in their

Operations room! Squadron Leader Hankey was worried because there was only one loo in the rest room. 'Don't worry, I have often been to France. It is always shared there.' He laughed.

'You have relieved me. We were all so worried you might be very proper, and demand a loo to yourself!' I had to move out of my room, and was billeted with the local tart, who had seen her best years, and whom I disliked upon sight. When I asked for a key, as I should be coming in late, she gave me a knowing look and a wink, and said, 'I know all about that too!' I was furious the next morning, returning from night duty, to find my brush and comb and make-up missing. I went to her room and knocked. She was still in bed.

'I have just come off night duty, I have to go to the camp for breakfast, I want to see all my possessions returned by my return, or I report you to the police!' I left her spluttering. I went into breakfast in a rage. I was always very touchy after night duty, one's eyes prickled, and any heartiness was most irritating. The Squadron Officer was just finishing. 'Good morning, ma'am, I have been put in billets with a tart and a thief!' I told her my story with venom! I was moved the next day to a very nice woman in some little house along the road. Her husband was abroad in the army, and she could not do enough for me. The only drawback was the loo at the end of the garden, very chilly in the snow. Two weeks later Elizabeth Stone arrived, and we became great friends. Liz hated night duty too, and would snarl at the hearty Admin. Officers when we came off duty at breakfast time! We had great fun doing this. It let off a lot of steam. Most of our controllers had been either stockbrokers or barristers, and grilled us on any information we gave them. Liz would get very cross when her evidence was doubted, and argue with great heat. In spite of differences on duty, we were all very happy together.

A young scientist I had known at Stanmore, was the resident expert, and I asked him to tell me in plain language the technicalities I had learned on my course. I had found some of the scientific symbols quite beyond me! It was a great help, and he was so kind and explained with great patience. It certainly helped me, and I felt sure for the first time on the information I gave. One evening I was approached by Tony Hankey and my scientist, always known by his initials, DC. 'Mitzi, I know you have nearly done a full duty, but would you slip off now and have supper, and return. We have a rather special operation on tonight, and I would like you to be in charge of the table?' I agreed. It was the bombing of the dams and all the top brass of the Group came and watched. It was very nerve-racking. There was an interval of waiting, and I reported a low number of aircraft returning. It was questioned, but sadly it was true.

It was only when my scientist friend was posted overseas that we realised, too late, that we were in love, but that is war.

Liz was now engaged to marry her HLI Lieutenant, David Taylor, and she had visited his parents in Glasgow. We went into Nottingham together after duty, to try to find some things for her trousseau. After shopping we had a coffee at a small café in an alley. A middle-aged woman came to our table. 'May I sit here?'

'Certainly.'

'Are you at Watnall?'

Instantly I was on the alert, and gave Liz a kick under the table. She looked at me, and I signed "look out" with my eyes. Liz was on it in a flash! 'Oh yes, we are.'

'How many WAAFs are there?'

'About four thousand,' said Liz.

'What do you do?'

'We cook meals.'

'What do the others do?'

'Clean aircraft!' Liz smiled sweetly.

'Do you live here?'

'Oh yes, have done for years.'

'When is the goose fair?'

'In July.'

'We must rush now we have to prepare our cooking!'

When we were alone I said, 'She is a spy."

'Of course she is. She didn't know when the Goose fair is held.' We went straight to the Adjutant's office and gave an exact description of the woman, and reported our conversation. Two days later they picked her up trying the same thing, and she was arrested as a spy. We were very pleased.

Liz was worried she had not heard from David for a month. "On my next fifty-six hours leave I am going to Colchester to find out if he is all right.' We went to London together, and I left her to go home. When I returned there was no sign of her. I went on duty. Still no Liz. I was starting to panic. My Sergeant, Dawn Lambert, said, Ma'am can you take a call from ASO Stone?'

'Liz, where are you?'

'I am at King's Cross, I have David in an ambulance. He is dying and I am taking him to Glasgow in a sleeper, I shall ring

Watnall Hall

you from there.'

'What shall I tell the Controller?'

'It's a matter of life and death!' The Controller was very kind, but the WAAF CO was livid.

'Tell ASO Stone to return at once!'

Liz came all the way back from Glasgow, reported to the Camp Commander, who immediately gave her compassionate leave. She told me that she had found David in the Military Hospital in Colchester, his whole body covered with running sores of eczema, in a thoroughly toxic condition. She went to the officer commanding. 'Sir, I am removing my fiancé from this hospital. He is in a dreadful condition, and I shall take him by ambulance to King's Cross and arrange a sleeper ambulance to Glasgow. I am a qualified VAD and I shall nurse him.'

'You do so at your own risk.'

'To me there is no choice. He will certainly die here!' It took five nurses seven hours to clean David when he arrived at the nursing home. His parents were horrified at his state, and very grateful to Liz. She went straight back to Glasgow and stayed ten days until

David was out of danger. By this time the WAAF Officers had been moved to Watnall Hall, and were all under the same roof. When Liz returned she said, 'Oh Mitz my throat is sore, will you have a look?' It looked ghastly, with white spots on the red inflamation!'

'You must report sick at once, I do not like the look of it.' She had diptheria!

The Senior Medical officer, Group Captain McAleer, was a good friend of all the WAAF officers, and would take any of us off duty to concerts in Nottingham. He took charge of Liz's case, and made it easy for me to visit the Isolation Hospital. I was the go-between, and David would ring me from Glasgow, and I would go to the hospital and relay their messages. It left Liz with paralyzed legs. She was invalided out of the WAAF, and David was discharged from the Army. They married that Summer, and I was their bridesmaid.

We now had a large underground Operations room, and many more WAAF Officers. Jane Salisbury-Jones and Sheila Wilson were in Ops 2, and I had known them at Stanmore. We were all good friends. I met an RAF Officer from their section called Johnnie Clyne or Cheers, because he always said that when he had a drink! He was a large man, over six feet, and quite heavy. He was a great party man who loved to come to our parties, and was very good to me. He would invite me to the cinema, and always gave me a box of Egyptian Abdullah cigarettes, which I liked, and a bunch of violets, which embarrassed me in uniform. He never smoked, but always carried a lighter. He was very kind and generous. I would say, 'You know I am a snake, Cheers. I don't love you, why do you go on taking me out?'

'Angel, it gives me such pleasure!' So we left it at that.

I was sent to an out station with another WAAF Officer. They thought we were from HQ and put us in damp sheets. I tried to sleep in my dressing-gown, but the East coast in winter is cold. When I returned to the Mess I felt odd, so I went to bed early before going on duty. I was expecting my friend Betty Wix to wake me. I thought I heard someone come into my room and I opened my eyes. In the glow of the electric fire I saw a figure in a cloak and top hat approaching my bed! At first I thought it was someone fooling about, but as it drew near a rush of icy air blew over me. I was stiff with fear. It stood with its arm out over me in the bed. I thought, 'Don't shout. You're grown up, pull the light cord.' After what seemed ages I managed to do it. NOTHING WAS THERE!

I was so afraid I left the light on until Betty came to wake me. I told her what had happened. 'Too much gin!' she said, laughing. In the morning I saw Frances, Lady Maude's housekeeper, in the hall. I retold my story. She smiled, 'Don't worry about that, Miss Ward. That was Lord Byron. He used to visit his first love here, Mary of Annesley. We see him about all the time. Last week an airman saw him in the drive. Thought it was someone in a gas cape, had quite a turn when he disappeared.'

I went on duty the next night. My neck swelled and by morning I was unable to fasten my collar. I was very ill with a high temperature, and unable to keep the M & B drug down. I dreaded the nights, such dreadful nightmares. The Air Force wrote to Freddie and Jane. 'Your daughter is very ill with a fever. We do not expect her to live.' They received the letter on Christmans Eve. On the day I was taken into Nottingham City hospital, the MO had noticed a white spot on my arm. I had glandular fever. The nurses came round with candles carol singing. It made me very homesick, and tears rolled down my cheeks. The next day the Sister said, 'You have a visitor.'

It was Cheers, with a basked full of fruit and a half bottle of champagne. 'Now, Angel, you must drink this. It will soon put you right!'

Sister, who was from Aberdeen, agreed with him. 'It will send up your temperature but it might do the trick.'

It did, I never looked back. The C of E minister came to my bed. 'Are you ready to meet your Maker?'

I was so cross. 'No, I'm bloody well not!' He left quickly. The RC padre came every night and told me funny stories, which was much more agreeable. To my great surprise and joy, Freddie came to see me. He stayed at "The Black Boy Hotel". Cheers was delighted to look after him. He told me later he still had doubts that I would live when he saw me, I looked so ill. I was in hospital two months. After sick leave Jane and Sheila invited me to share a cottage with them at the gates to Watnall Hall. Although rather primitive, overrun with mice, and the odd toad in the primitive kitchen, we found it a relief to be away from the horde of WAAF Officers in Watnall Hall.

Before we left, we arranged for the officers of our favourite bomber squadron based at Waddington to come and dine at Watnall Hall. I went to Lady Maude, the owner of the Hall. She was eighty-five years old, and very kind to us all. It was great fun to go to tea with her, and hear her stories of being presented to

Queen Victoria, and staying at Buckingham Palace. She married Sir Launcelot, and went to the Boer War with him as a nurse. She thought the present war a non-event! I asked her if she would lend me the family silver, explaining that these men flew over Germany at great peril, and we wanted to give them a peace-time dinner party.

'Certainly, on one condition, that I am allowed to see the table when it is set.'

I readily promised. We held it in the White Drawing room, which had mirrored walls, and the reflection of all the silver and candelabra was wonderful to see. We had arranged great bowls of roses from the garden, and a delicious dinner. Our guests were struck dumb when they saw the gleaming table. True to my word, I went for Lady Maude. She was in her dressing-gown, and came down stairs to see our efforts. She shed a few tears and congratulated us. 'Will you help me to bed?'

'Of course, Lady Maude.'

We went upstairs, and I helped her into her four-poster bed. 'You know, dear, when Sir Launcelot was alive, I only had one hot water bottle, now I have to have three!' I thought how strange life's equations can become!

It was a very special evening, and the guests were so delighted they treated Jane, Sheila and me to a night at "The White Hart Hotel" in Lincoln, and dinner in their mess.

We were invited to a local squire's house for a party. It was very lavish, and at the buffet I looked across the table. An Army Officer of high rank was regarding me quizzically. I smiled. He came and joined me, and when we had chosen our food, we sat down together. 'My name is Colin, you have been fascinating me since you arrived. Tell me about yourself.'

'I am Mitzi, and am stationed at HQ up the road. I come from Bickley in Kent.' We had a great chat. I found he was married with two children, and a very glamorous wife and I was shown photographs. 'Are you engaged?'

'No, my boyfriends either get killed or go overseas!'

'So I am in luck!'

'I wonder what you mean?'

'Well, you won't object to my escorting you to dances, will you?'

'I do not have affairs with married men. As long as you understand that, I should be delighted!' He laughed. His eyes had nice creases at the corners. 'Let's dance.'

We became good friends, and I was careful not to be alone with him on dark nights, because I was sure his intentions were not exactly honourable!

We decided to give a dinner party in our cottage. We persuaded Lady Maude's cook at Watnall Hall to prepare a duck for us and the whole thing was a great success. Jane's beau, a Polish Wing commander, came and Sheila asked a friend called Blenner Hassett, who adored her, but it was not reciprocated, and I asked Colin. He came with a bottle of whisky, which was like gold-dust then. 'I told the bar officer it was for my old mother!' We all roared with laughter, and I promised to write a letter thanking him, which I did in wobbly writing.

On duty we were very busy, sending a thousand bombers a night to Germany, and now the American Air Force went on daylight raids. Some of the Bomber Group officers paid us a visit, and I was asked to show them round, and explain how we worked, which I did. On the way back in the staff car I sat between the Group Captain and the Wing Commander. To my horror I felt a hand sliding from each side along my back. Of course they met! 'Sorry, sir,' said the Wing Commander, rapidly drawing his hand away. I just laughed, and they all joined in.

I had a telephone call from London. My scientist sweetheart had returned from overseas after two years. Would I please stay calm and meet him on my next leave. Memories of our short and poignant love affair went through my head. We had discovered the week he was posted we were in love. We had lunch together in the RAF Mess, and went to their ante-room where he played Chopin to me. We wandered back to Watnall Hall and promised to keep in touch. 'Why not come to our dance next weekend if you are still here?' To my joy he drove up in his old green Bentley, arriving about 10 pm. He was not a good dancer, so we mostly sat and chatted. When we said "Goodnight" we kissed with feeling. We spent the next day together, and then he had to leave. It really hurt. 'Always ring this number when you come on leave, I may still be there.' We met once again on a very wet day in London, and wandered round Leicester Square, not noticing the rain at all. He was such fun to be with, very witty, and mocked sentimentality of any kind. He took me to Euston and put me on the train. The next time I rang he had left. Now he had returned. I was in turmoil. How would it be? My next fifty-six hours was at the weekend. I arranged to meet him at Euston and arranged to stay with my friend Margaret Chinery in Maida Vale. When I saw him he had aged. With the strain of war in the Middle East, his hair was grey, and the boyish charm had gone. A serious man met me, and we shook hands. We spoke of normal things, people we both knew. I asked about his experiences abroad. He seemed reluctant to discuss them. We went to a Somerset Maughan trilogy at the cinema. He took me to dinner to a small restaurant in Leicester Square. There we began to feel more at ease, and he began to joke, and make his brand of semi-shocking statements. 'Out of the goodness of your heart would you come back to "The Park Lane Hotel" with me?'

I had a moment of panic, but was reassured when he continued, 'There are so many tarts in Piccadilly I shall never get back without an escort!' We went out into the blackout, and with the aid of his torch found our way to "The Park Lane Hotel". 'It has been wonderful to see you again, ring me on your next leave.' I returned to Margaret in Maida Vale. It was very difficult to find my way in the blackout, and luckily some people came out of a pub, and I was able to get my bearings. Margaret had been at Stanmore with me, but had left when the option came up. She designed theatrical costumes for Motley. 'How was it?'

'Not very good, we have both changed.' I am glad it was never possible for us to become lovers, and I can always treasure the joyous feeling of being in love, and being loved, the sorrow of parting, and have no regrets. We talked for an hour, and went to bed.

It was Christmas week, and Jane and Sheila and I thought we would give a cocktail party before our Christmas fancy dress party in the Mess, on December the 29th. It was deep snow, and getting on and off duty was difficult. I told Jane I was to be on duty Christmas Eve. 'I do the 8 pm to midnight watch. Shall we go to early service?'

'OK I shall be in before you, and will have cocoa ready, so that you can get to bed quickly.' I went out into the bitter night, and trudged down the road thinking about all the recent events. I wondered what the next year would bring.

18

Christmas Day, 1943

Charles McCall stretched himself in bed. The snow was thick round the window pane. His batman knocked, 'Happy Christmas, sir. It's Christmas card weather!'

'You are right there, it is cold enough to freeze the balls off a brass monkey!' Laughing, the batman switched on the electric fire.

Charles lay thinking for a while. It was Christmas day and the English always make such a fuss. In Scotland it is New Year's Eve, Hogmanay, which is the great celebration. He smiled to himself, thinking of parties in the past at the Art College. He thought of his last leave, painting the portrait of his blonde girlfriend, of her violet eyes, and curvaceous body. He sighed and, slowly clambering out of bed, bathed and dressed himself in his best uniform. His "Sam Browne" was gleaming, ready to put on when he went out. That batman was good. His buttons were brilliant, must give him a Christmas bonus.

He went to breakfast. "Guns", the fellow whose office he shared, was at the table. 'Happy Christmas, Mac.'

'Same to you, Guns. Are you on this "serving the troops lark"?'

'Impossible to get out of, if one is around.'

At that moment Major Phil Mayhew walked into the Mess. 'I have come to invite you to drinks in our Mess at "The Horse and Groom". I can give you a lift, I only have a WAAF with me at the moment.'

Charles grinned. 'Sounds very nourishing, I should like that!'

'Right, I shall leave in ten minutes.' McCall went back to his room, and put on his "Sam Browne" and his heavy greatcoat, picked up his cap, and went to the jeep parked at the front door. A WAAF Sergeant jumped out, very dark hair, flushed red cheeks. 'Good morning, sir! Happy Christmas! I am Dawn Lambert.'

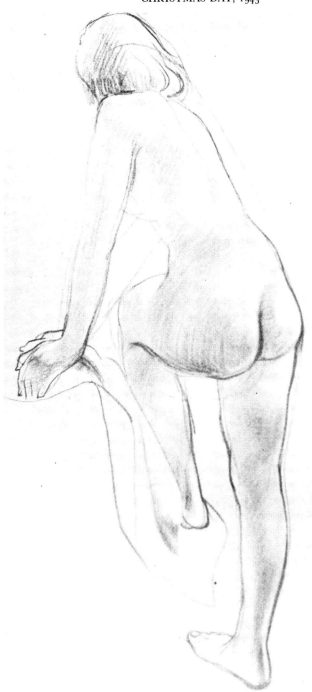

Nude, drawn at the Edinburgh College of Art by Charles McCall

'I am Charles McCall. It seems to be a good start to the day!' He climbed into the back of the jeep. The Major came out, swinging himself into the driver's seat. 'Off we go then. The party is due to start at 10 am, so that we have time for drinks before the Christmas celebrations start.' The jeep roared off up the snowy road, passing the RAF Camp and Watnall Hall. Reaching the top of a very steep hill, they saw three figures ahead of them. Dawn said, 'It's two of my officers, let's give them a lift.' They drew up alongside the group. Flight Lieutenant MacLaren, the RAF liason officer, saluted the party. 'Well met. We are just coming to your drinks bash, I thought I would bring Mitzi and Jane.'

'Wonderful. Hop in, and we'll give you a lift!'

Charles climbed out to let them get to the back bench. Mac said, 'Charles meet Jane Salisbury-Jones, and Mitzi Ward. This is Charles McCall. he is our Camouflage officer, known as "Deceipt and Deception". Everyone laughed. McCall looked at the two young women. The red-haird one was very pretty in a snooty English way, but the dark girl was *very* interesting: nicely rounded, with great dark brown eyes that shone, high cheek bones, very bedable!

That is a face I MUST paint.

They arrived at the Mess.

Epilogue

The sad Indian "Mystic Man of the East" had indeed given me great value for a shilling, when he told me in 1936 I should meet and marry an artist! It all came true, and in my book *Interior with Figure* the story is told.

Freddie lived to eighty-six years of age, repaying all his debts, and enjoying his last years in Chelsea, working to within a month of his death.

I should like to have described my work with the RAF in greater detail as it was fascinating and rewarding work. Sadly, it still remains an Official Secret within the Act, so all I could do was to hint at what occurred.

Charles McCall proved my reason for living. His paintings, many of me, are all over the world, so he achieved his wish to paint me! Much more than that, he lived to see his work appreciated. By surviving on his work alone, never teaching, as advised when young, he achieved the standard of art that caught the eye of collectors. We both saluted the courage of early collectors who trusted their judgement when his work was unknown — also the Galleries and Government Art Collection who bought his work.

I thank the Good Lord for the gift of the two most important men in my life, and for the good friends who gave it loving friendship, excitement, colour and humour.

Sadly Charles became ill in April 1989 and died suddenly on the 3rd of October the same year. It leaves me with a great sorrow but also a deep thankfulness for all our wonderful years together.

LIST OF ILLUSTRATIONS